WILLIAM MORRIS
AND THE ARTS AND CRAFTS HOME

WILLIAM MORRIS
AND THE ARTS AND CRAFTS HOME

by PAMELA TODD
photographs by CHRIS TUBBS

CHRONICLE BOOKS

SAN FRANCISCO

PAGE 1: This photograph of William Morris, taken in 1876, was used as the frontispiece to *The Collected Works of William Morris*, edited by his daughter May.

PAGE 2: A view through to one of the attic bedrooms at William Morris's Kelmscott Manor.

PAGE 3: Illustration from the title page of *A Book of Verse* by William Morris.

OPPOSITE (TOP TO BOTTOM): The garden room at Houghton Manor (page 128); a child's bedroom at the Morgan house in Wales (page 136); the parlor at Poole's Corner in Rockland, Massachusetts (page 146); the living room at a country mansion near Plymouth, Massachusetts (page 152); the entrance hall at an Arts & Crafts farmhouse in Suffolk (page 162); the garden studio in a Victorian terraced house in London (page 170).

First published in the United States in 2005 by Chronicle Books LLC.

Main text copyright © 2005 by Pamela Todd.
Case Studies text © 2005 by Palazzo Editions Limited.
Photographs copyright © 2005 by Chris Tubbs, except as noted on page 188, which constitutes a continuation of the copyright page.

Library of Congress Cataloging-in-Publication Data available.

ISBN 0-8118-4275-4

Manufactured in Singapore.

Created and produced for Chronicle Books by
Palazzo Editions Limited
15 Gay Street,
Bath, BA1 2PH
United Kingdom

Book Designer: David Fordham
Picture Researcher: Emily Hedges and David Penrose
Managing Editor: Victoria Webb
Text for the case studies written by Caroline Ball.
Additional material for the list of suppliers and places to visit edited by John Burrows.

Distributed in Canada by Raincoast Books
9050 Shaughnessy Street
Vancouver, British Columbia V6P 6E5

10 9 8 7 6 5 4 3 2 1

Chronicle Books LLC
85 Second Street
San Francisco, California 94105

www.chroniclebooks.com

CONTENTS

INTRODUCTION

"If I were asked to say what is at once the most

important production of Art and the thing

most to be longed for, I should answer,

A beautiful House."

WILLIAM MORRIS, "SOME THOUGHTS ON THE ORNAMENTED
MANUSCRIPTS OF THE MIDDLE AGES," 1894

LEFT: The window seat in the bay of the first-floor drawing room at Red House afforded William and Jane Morris splendid views of the orchard and surrounding Kent countryside.

ABOVE RIGHT: The twenty-three-year-old William Morris, a "slight figure" in those days, according to his great friend Edward Burne-Jones.

"I HALF WISH that I had not been born with a sense of romance and beauty in this accursed age," William Morris, the forerunner of modern design, wrote to his friend and confidante Georgiana Burne-Jones in the year 1895. Morris was born in Walthamstow, England, in 1834. As a young man, he began to lament the industrialization and mass-production of the Victorian era, which he believed had impoverished craftsmen and resulted in shoddy, uninspiring work. The idea of starting his own business was prompted by the dearth of well-designed furniture and furnishings available in Great Britain, the responsibilities of family life, and his own lack of a proper profession.

Morris's career trajectory, as set out in a long lively letter to an Austrian friend, had begun in 1853 at Exeter College, Oxford, where his plans to enter the church had been "corrected" by the ideas of the social commentator and art critic John Ruskin. It continued, during 1856-7, in the architectural offices of G. E. Street, where he met Philip Webb, and currently rested, somewhat precariously, in the fields of art and poetry. While his friends had embarked on definite career paths—Edward Burne-Jones and Dante Gabriel Rossetti as painters, and Philip Webb as an architect—Morris's own occupation was still undefined.

Morris's first book of poetry, *The Defence of Guenevere* (1858), had not been a commercial success. Although he was a man of independent means, the income from the shares he had inherited in Devon Great Consuls was prone to fluctuation and had declined

LEFT: Morris's "Cray" pattern for printed textiles (1884).

RIGHT: The title page of *A Book of Verse* by William Morris. Morris put together this illustrated collection of fifty-one of his own poems as a thirtieth birthday present for his dear friend Georgiana Burne-Jones. He was responsible for all the calligraphy and most of the border decorations, though various friends helped. Charles Fairfax Murray painted the portrait of Morris at the center of this page.

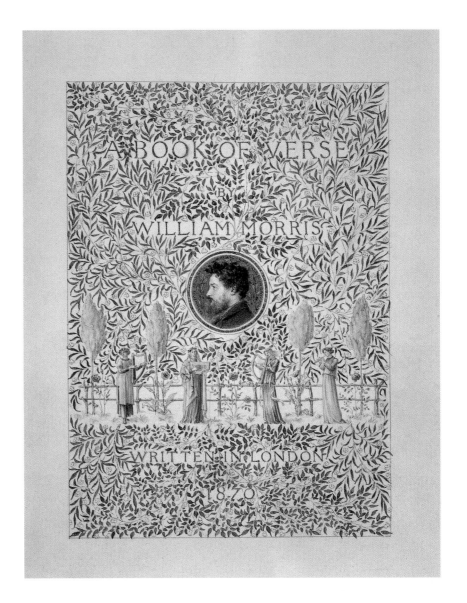

dramatically over three years, from the considerable sum of £819 in 1857, to £572 in 1860, the year that he had spent £4,000 on what became known as Red House, in Kent. Morris had commissioned Webb to design the house for him and his wife, Jane Burden, whom he had married in 1859. With the prospect of parenthood on the horizon, he needed to establish a reliable source of income.

In the spring of 1861, having decided that all the minor arts were in a state of "complete degradation" and having experienced the difficulty of finding good furnishings for Red House, Morris decided "with the conceited courage of a young man" to "set up a sort of shop," where he and six friends could produce and sell painted furniture, stained glass, and embroidered and decorative articles. "The firm," as it was informally known, consisted of William Morris, his best man Charles Faulkner, his best friend Edward Burne-Jones, whom he had met at Oxford, the architect Philip Webb, and three

other close friends: Dante Gabriel Rossetti, a member of the Pre-Raphaelite Brotherhood, founded in 1848; Peter Paul Marshall, a Scottish engineer and amateur painter; and the artist Ford Madox Brown. Morris, Marshall, Faulkner & Co., Fine Art Workmen in Painting, Carving, Furniture and Metals, came into being on April 11, 1861, with £100 of financial backing provided by Morris's mother, and a nominal investment of £1 from each of the seven partners.

The firm set up at 8 Red Lion Square, London, with a showroom and offices on the first floor, a kiln in the basement, and the workshops, which Rossetti referred to as "the Topsaic laboratory" (in reference to Morris's nickname of "Topsy," acquired because of his wild curls and generally tousled appearance), housed in the attics on the third floor. Here, Morris strove to evoke the spirit of a medieval workshop, where there was pride in work and joy in craftsmen working together. Practical jokes were played—usually on Morris, whose explosive

LEFT: A caricature of William Morris bent over his loom, presenting his back to the audience who have come to hear him lecture on weaving, by Edward Burne-Jones (*c.* 1880).

temper the others loved to provoke. The mood was optimistic and egalitarian. Morris recruited youths from the Industrial Home for Destitute Boys on Euston Road, which had been set up in 1858 to teach them trades, and friends and family were also enlisted.

Morris believed in the ideal of woman as co-worker, and at the firm men and women worked alongside one another in a heady atmosphere of emancipation and equality. The work was hard, but Morris's enthusiasm was infectious, and, despite Philip Webb's assertion that business was conducted "like a picnic," the firm flourished. In a letter to Andreas Scheu, Morris wrote, "We made some progress before long, though we were naturally much ridiculed. I took the matter up as a business and began in the teeth of difficulties not easy to imagine to make some money in it."

Rossetti had envisaged "a shop like Giotto!" and "a sign on the door," and the contrast between the dim interior of the firm's first-floor showroom and the new dazzling department stores springing up in the West End of London was marked. Shops that would later become household names, such as Frederick Gamage's on Buckingham Palace Road, the Army and Navy stores in Victoria, and John Lewis on Oxford Street, had just begun to make an appearance. Liberty's would soon open on Regent Street. These great emporiums of luxury, with their ostentatious displays, set out to entice customers, while curious visitors to the showroom on the first floor of Red Lion Square found themselves in a shadowy space filled with "bewildering treasures," which Morris, dressed in his blue worker's shirt and round hat, and with dirty hands, would show them with the impatient air of a busy man torn from something else that he would much rather be doing. Boosted by such idiosyncrasies, business boomed. Rossetti noticed how Morris's "very eccentricities and independent attitude towards his patrons seems to have drawn [them] around him."

Henry James considered Morris an impressive figure: "He is short, burly, corpulent, very careless and unfinished in his dress," he told his sister Alice, in a letter written in March 1869. "He has a very loud voice and a nervous restless manner and a perfectly unaffected and business-like address. His talk is wonderfully to the point and remarkable for clear good sense. . . He's an extraordinary example, in short, of a delicate sensitive genius and taste, saved by a perfectly healthy body and temper." James was extremely impressed by Morris's "exquisite" taste: "everything he has and does is superb and beautiful," he insisted.

Morris turned out to be a creative shopkeeper who made and sold the things he himself would like to buy, and he went against the grain of the age by getting to grips with the manual labor involved, never designing anything he could not make himself. He wanted "to revive a sense of beauty in home life, to restore the dignity of art to ordinary household decoration," and his hobbies of wood carving and embroidery held him in good stead at the firm as he rapidly combined his genius for design with an emerging talent for business.

ABOVE: The firm's highly prestigious commission to design the Green Dining Room (1866–7) for the South Kensington Museum came from the museum's progressive director, Henry Cole. Edward Burne-Jones designed the stained glass and gilded panels, taking the months of the year as his theme. Philip Webb designed the ceiling and frieze for what is now known as the William Morris Room in the Victoria and Albert Museum.

Before long the firm was producing a comprehensive textile range, from handwoven tapestries and carpets to embroideries, printed textiles, and woven fabrics, as well as mural decorations, architectural carvings, stained glass, metalwork, ceramics, furniture, and light fittings.

With the help of a persuasive prospectus and the serendipitous timing of the International Exhibition of 1862, held in South Kensington, which provided a platform for the first public showing of the firm's work, Morris succeeded in attracting substantial commissions from the Church of England, St. James's Palace, and the South Kensington Museum (now the Victoria and Albert Museum). For the Exhibition, he created a "Medieval Court," a great novelty in a predominantly modern and industrial exhibition, which included a sofa

by Rossetti and six of his own pieces, including a cabinet painted with scenes from the life of St. George, as well as screens, embroidered hangings, chests, chairs, an inlaid escritoire, and bookcases.

The popular press had a field day. "Pre-Raffaelitism has descended from art to manufacture," trumpeted the *Illustrated Exhibitor*. *The Building News* complained that the pieces were "no more adapted to the wants of living men, than mediaeval armour would be to modern warfare, middle-aged cookery to civic feasts, or Norman oaths to an English lady's drawing-room." Some of the other exhibitors even accused the partners of touching up old stained glass and passing it off as their own work. Despite all the sniping and the criticism, plenty of pieces sold, and the firm had further orders for painted cabinets, plain black-stained chairs, and serge and cotton embroidered hangings, as well as considerable interest in Morris's first designs for wallpapers and tiles.

What Morris offered was not just a style eagerly embraced by a swathe of the populace, from country house to suburbia

ABOVE: The elaborate "St. George's Cabinet" was one of the firm's showpieces at the International Exhibition of Art and Industry in 1862. Philip Webb designed the cabinet, using mahogany, oak, and pine, but it was Morris himself who decorated the gilded surface with scenes from the legend of St. George. It was priced at 50 guineas but, despite attracting some favorable attention, it failed to sell.

RIGHT: A watercolor drawing by Lexden Lewis Pocock, entitled *The Pond at Merton Abbey*, showing Morris's weaving, tapestry, and fabric printing works in the background.

(and especially the growing middle class, made prosperous by the booming Victorian economy), but quite simply a way of life. The firm offered a complete range of products unified by Morris's own style and vision—by "my artistic knowledge and taste, *on which the whole of my business depends*," as he pointed out rather tetchily to Thomas Wardle when one of Wardle's dyers had disregarded his orders.

Despite Webb's early misgivings, Morris proved a born entrepreneur. Multi-talented and keen to try his hand at most things, he nevertheless grasped the importance of delegation and placed the running of the firm in the hands of competent managers. Morris, Marshall, Faulkner & Co. never sold merchandise at discount prices, and, unlike other high-class shops, they marked the price of each item clearly and expected prompt payment. Customers, some of whom were accustomed to treating tradesmen's bills with disdain, were politely informed that "all sums unpaid after one month from the delivery of the account will be charged with

interest at the rate of 5 per cent per annum." Morris never used advertising to persuade, but merely to describe, and in his lifetime he saw Morris & Co. (as it became known after a restructuring in March 1875, following the departure of Rossetti and Madox Brown) grow into a flourishing and fashionable interior-decorating firm, particularly renowned for its wallpapers and textiles. Morris himself was so much in demand that, by the 1880s, in order to "stop fools and impertinents," he felt obliged to ration his time and charged extravagant fees for personal visits to the homes of clients in London and elsewhere.

Over time, the firm moved from Red Lion Square to Queen Square, taking showrooms at the fashionable end of Oxford Street (later moving from there to the equally fashionable shopping district of George Street, Hanover Square) and diversified and expanded. Morris converted workshops for printing, glassmaking, weaving, and dyeing on the banks of the River Wandle at Merton Abbey, Surrey. He collaborated with

Thomas Wardle, who ran a dye-house in Leek, in Staffordshire, where he experimented with vegetable dyes culled from old herbals and medieval treatises, boiling twigs and the crushed carcasses of insects in his quest for more subtle colors for his chintz designs. He set up a workshop to make hand-knotted "Hammersmith" carpets in a converted coach house adjacent to Kelmscott House, his Hammersmith home, and made daily visits to the embroideresses working under his daughter May's instruction at her house, at 8 Hammersmith Terrace.

Morris believed that employers had a moral obligation to ensure that each worker took "pleasure in his work," and that . . .

> "... decent conditions of light and breathing-space and cleanliness shall surround him, that he shall be made to feel himself not the brainless 'hand' but the intelligent cooperator, the *friend* of the man who directs his labour, that his honest toil shall inevitably win fair and comfortable wages, whatever be the low-water record of the market-price of men, that illness or trouble befalling him during his term of employment shall not mean dismissal or starvation."

Such fair-handed generosity, coupled with an insistence on using only the best materials, made Morris's work expensive, and, in the light of his subsequent zeal for socialism, it saddened and occasionally enraged him that his best work became the exclusive province of the wealthy. On one occasion, his famous temper flared, and he complained loudly about having to "spend my life in ministering to the swinish luxury of the rich!" The promise made in the firm's original prospectus, that "good decoration, involving rather the luxury of taste than the luxury of costliness, will be found to be much less expensive than is generally supposed," had not been kept. However, high standards of design and finish were central to Morris's notion of good work, and it was this refusal to compromise that ensured his continuing reputation and led to the enduring success of his work, up to the present day. "There is no excuse," he wrote, "for doing anything which is not strikingly beautiful."

Over the course of his lifetime, Morris harnessed his considerable energies to a number of causes, including conservation, the lot of the poor, and the revival of old printing techniques. He was an ardent politician and social reformer, and formed the Hammersmith Socialist League in 1884, advocating a workers' revolution. He also

ABOVE: The last and most expensive of Morris's elaborate repeat patterns for printed textiles, "Cray" was designed in 1884, and available in cotton or linen.

ABOVE RIGHT: Morris & Co. employees printing chintz with hand blocks at Merton Abbey, where the firm's workshop relocated in 1881.

established the Society for the Protection of Ancient Buildings in 1877 and set up the Kelmscott Press in 1891.

Most significantly, Morris was the spiritual leader and, together with John Ruskin and the architect Augustus Pugin, one of the great founding fathers of the Arts & Crafts Movement, which redefined the role of art and craftsmanship, and underpinned many of the social reforms that flowed from it. The Movement shared Morris's commitment to inclusivity and creating opportunities for women, who found in its revival of traditional techniques such as embroidery, weaving, and enameling, an outlet for their creativity and a respectable way of earning a living. However, gender still determined the division of labor, with men dominating fields such as metalwork and furniture production as well as architecture, and women working hard to create a niche for themselves in areas such as needlework, bookbinding, and pottery.

The roots of the Arts & Crafts Movement can be traced back to the Great Exhibition, held at Crystal Palace in 1851, and to the dismayed and disgusted reaction of the young Morris and his friends to the "wonderful ugliness" of the mass-produced exhibits on show, which they believed were devoid of any soul and dehumanized the workers who made them. What began as a return to the styles and

manners of the medieval period—its cathedrals, furnishings, costumes, and, crucially, its workers' guilds—developed, under the inspiration and guidance of Morris, to embrace more day-to-day handicrafts.

The unashamedly "artistic" homes, gardens, and products of the Arts & Crafts Movement celebrated the individuality of the craftsmen and craftswomen who made them. At its most romantic and intense, the Movement offered a complete, if rigorous, model for living, which Morris himself mapped out in his Utopian novel *News from Nowhere* (1890), and which exponents like Charles Ashbee and Elbert Hubbard, among others, sought to put into practice in communal communities in the Cotswolds and in East Aurora, New York. The Movement was attractive to many disenchanted by rapid industrialization. Its influences, both social and aesthetic, were felt in continental Europe, where ideas cross-fertilized, returning to Great Britain enriched and enlivened, and in the United States, where its ideals were enthusiastically embraced and adapted.

ABOVE: The frontispiece (by Charles March Gere) and first page of Morris's *News from Nowhere*, a Utopian romance, published in instalments in *The Commonweal* between January and October 1890, and inspired by Kelmscott Manor and the surrounding countryside.

OPPOSITE LEFT: Printing blocks made from pear-tree wood, showing two pairs of birds, used in the production of "Strawberry Thief" (1883).

OPPOSITE RIGHT: A trial fent for "Iris" printed cotton, designed in 1876, showing the registration stamp. Morris always referred to this pattern as "Flower de luce."

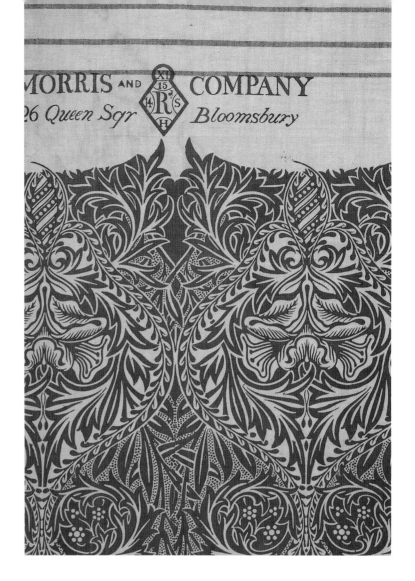

The Arts & Crafts Movement acquired its name in 1888, when William Morris's tapestries, William de Morgan's tiles, Walter Crane's wallpapers and Edward Burne-Jones's stained glass went on show on October 4 at the New Gallery in London, along with other work by the newly formed Arts & Crafts Exhibition Society. The show was a success and drew enthusiastic reviews. *The Builder* reported that it was "full of things which seem to have been done because the designer enjoyed doing them," even if it found some of the exhibits a little "outré and eccentric." Walter Crane set out the Society's mission statement "to turn our artists into craftsmen and craftsmen into artists" in the catalog to that first exhibition. Humble, plain, honest furniture such as that designed by Ford Madox Brown for Morris & Co. sold alongside more ornate "Arthurian" pieces, but each had in common the individuality of the craftsmanship and the vision behind it of beauty and harmony that harked back to the rules and methods of the medieval guild system. Like Morris, Arts & Crafts practitioners truly believed that the quality of life for everyone would be improved if only integrity could be restored to the everyday objects in daily use.

At the heart of the Movement was Morris's idealization of the rural idyll. "Suppose," he wrote to Edward Burne-Jones's sister-in-law, Louisa Baldwin, "people lived in little communities among gardens and green fields, so that you could be in the country in five minutes' walk, and had few wants, almost no furniture for instance, and no servants, and studied the (difficult) arts of enjoying life, and finding out what they really wanted: then I think that one might hope civilisation had really begun."

Morris was a romantic and a revolutionary who wanted to reform the world, to make life more beautiful, simple, and satisfying for more people. He stressed the connection between art and life, work and enjoyment, and promoted the ideal of domestic happiness, without, sadly, achieving it himself. He was, inevitably, compromised by contradictions. A socialist who lived in two large houses, one in London and the other outside Lechlade, linked by the river Thames. An intense romantic whose marriage to the ideal beauty he had, in true courtly fashion, rescued from the dragon of poverty, was blighted by the betrayal of her love for one of his best friends, Dante Gabriel Rossetti. He found consistency in work, and during his life "did more work than that of ten men," according to his doctor, who, in October 1896, attributed the cause of his death, aged 62, to "simply being William Morris."

THE SUSSEX RUSH-SEATED CHAIRS

MORRIS AND COMPANY

449 OXFORD STREET, LONDON, W.

"ROSSETTI" ARM-CHAIR.
IN BLACK, 16/6.

SUSSEX CORNER CHAIR.
IN BLACK, 10/6.

SUSSEX SINGLE CHAIR.
IN BLACK, 7/-.

SUSSEX ARM-CHAIR.
IN BLACK, 9/9.

ROUND-SEAT CHAIR.
IN BLACK, 10/6.

SUSSEX SETTEE, 4 FT. 6 IN. LONG.
IN BLACK, 35/-.

ROUND SEAT PIANO CHAIR.
IN BLACK, 10/6.

LEFT: A page from the Morris & Co. furniture catalog of about 1910, showing the firm's range of rush-seated Morris chairs.

RIGHT: Light floods into Jane Morris's "Willow" papered bedroom at Kelmscott Manor.

A true Renaissance man, Morris was so multitalented that Max Beerbohm famously remarked, "Of course he was a wonderful all-round man, but the act of walking round him always tired me." Morris's energy and capacity for hard work was famous, and the list of his accomplishments long and extraordinarily varied. When he died, he was remembered as a writer and poet (he had turned down the post of Poet Laureate on the death of Tennyson in 1892), as well as an artist and influential craftsman. In life, whenever he had been called upon to name his profession, he had chosen to style himself "Designer."

The profound impact of the "Morris school" on the development of European decorative design that had begun in Morris's lifetime—Morris & Co. had agents in Frankfurt, Berlin, and Paris (as well as New York, Boston, and Philadelphia)—continued to grow and influence the course of design. Today, William Morris is remembered most for his intricate and beguiling pattern designs, which, like his best epic poems, express his deep love of landscape and his strong feeling for history, nature, and season. Oscar Wilde called him "the greatest

handicraftsman we have had in England since the fourteenth century," but it is possible to trace Morris's impact on design right up to the birth of Modernism, and even beyond.

This book celebrates and explores Morris's genius for decoration and design and, by moving through the rooms of a house—from entrance hall to bathroom—shows how he envisaged and implemented schemes for interiors in his own homes and those of others, and how a modern audience can learn from and apply his guiding principles. Morris passionately believed that beautiful surroundings promoted creativity and happiness. "My work is the embodiment of dreams in one form or another," he wrote to a friend in July 1856, and romance and fantasy are often found in a William Morris interior. However, practicality and comfort are also present, and it is the two sides of Morris that make his vision of "how we might live" so compelling and attractive. In the chapters that follow, we explore Morris's guiding principles in order to inspire and enable a modern audience to recreate the Arts & Crafts style in their own homes.

CHAPTER ONE

THE OUTSIDE VIEW

THE EXTERIOR AND GARDENS

LEFT: This detail of the windows on the west front of Red House shows the originality and imagination Philip Webb brought to the design. The red bricks, laid in "English Bond," are perfectly complemented by the red-tiled roof.

ABOVE RIGHT: William Morris in his round hat and working smock, a costume adopted by his Arts & Crafts followers.

"Architecture would lead us to all the arts,

as it did with earlier men: but if we despise it

and take no note of how we are housed,

the other arts will have a hard time of it indeed."

WILLIAM MORRIS, "THE BEAUTY OF LIFE," 1880

In 1859, THE TWENTY-SIX-YEAR-OLD William Morris commissioned Philip Webb, a friend and progressive young architect who was very much in sympathy with his Pre-Raphaelite ideals, to design a house for himself and his beautiful teenage bride, Jane Burden. The idea for Red House had developed during a walking trip in France the previous year. It was Webb's first commission and very much a collaborative vision. Morris, who scribbled enthusiastic notes on the back of French train timetables, wanted a house "very medieval in spirit" that suited his personality and fitted in with the natural surroundings of the site at Upton (now Bexleyheath) in Kent; he wanted "a small Palace of Art of my own"—a reference to Tennyson's great poem in which the narrator builds himself an exquisite house "hung with arras green and blue."

The new house, which Dante Gabriel Rossetti fondly referred to as "The Towers of Topsy," rose in the midst of an orchard of apple and cherry trees. It was a deeply pleasing asymmetrical L-shaped house, made of warm red brick (hence its name) in a scaled-down Gothic style that incorporated a great arched entrance porch; steep, irregular gabled roofs topped with tall chimneys; and a weather vane ornamented with the initials "W. M." Morris's presence and personality were stamped throughout the house with his initials, and with mottoes such as *Ars Longa Vita Brevis* ("Life is short, but Art is long") and his personal statement *Si je puis* ("If I can"), which appears in embroideries and stained-glass windows.

Webb designed his buildings "as they should be," from the inside out, considering first the functional interior relationships of rooms to corridors and stairwells, and he adhered to the architect Augustus Pugin's principle of fidelity to place. Red House, attributed with breaking the classical mold, embraced the vernacular and sparked the revolution in domestic architecture that, for the next half a century, influenced succeeding generations of architects eager to put function first, relate their buildings to the landscape, and, most crucially, build them from carefully selected, often local, materials. It has been called the first Arts & Crafts building.

"It was not a large house," wrote the Morrises' good friend Georgiana Burne-Jones, "but purpose and proportion had been so skillfully observed in its design as to arrange for all reasonable demands and give an impression of ample space everywhere." Webb's original plan allowed for an extension—in effect another L-shaped building—that would enclose the charming cone-roofed well in the central courtyard and eventually double the living space,

FAR LEFT: Morris's "Daisy" wallpaper pattern (1864).

ABOVE: "More a poem than a house"— Red House, designed by Philip Webb in collaboration with William Morris in 1859, helped to change the direction of English domestic building, and proved to be enormously influential.

for Morris cherished a dream of establishing at Red House a Utopian community, a fellowship of like-minded creative friends. Until that plan could be realized, however, trellises thickly covered with roses filled the spaces, creating a romantic enclosed medieval garden at the center of which was the little well that, according to Georgiana, "summed up the feeling of the whole place."

Creating a congenial space in which to entertain friends was central to Morris's ideas of "How we Live and How we Might Live," described in a lecture series in 1885. Simplicity was a keynote. Morris detested the Victorian vogue for cluttered rooms where everything, including the piano, was draped in heavy layers, and a perpetual state of gloom was maintained by shrouding the windows in up to four layers of curtains, moving out from lace or muslin, through swathes of silk and satin, to damask and velvet. Morris welcomed the light that flooded into the house through windows of different shapes, sizes, and designs—round, arched, long, thin, rectangular, and often uncurtained.

Morris's strong love of England and excellent eye for authentic detail had developed early. As a dreamy and somewhat delicate child, whose imagination had been stoked by Sir Walter Scott's *Waverley* novels, he had spent part of his childhood trotting around Epping Forest on the pony provided by his indulgent parents, extravagantly attired in a miniature suit of armor, storing up details of the medieval architecture and design of the local Essex churches. The family lived at Woodford Hall, a Palladian mansion surrounded by a fifty-acre park and farm. Morris's father, who had made his wealth effortlessly through a fortunate investment in a Devon mining firm, was a keen medievalist and designed a coat of arms for the family. Morris grew up in a household that was run like a manor-house in the Middle Ages: beer was brewed, bread baked, butter churned, and the nine children sat down to a midday meal of cakes, cheese, and ale.

The third child and eldest boy of the family, Morris shared his father's deep love of Arthurian legend and became a great romantic visionary, emotionally anchored in the chivalric tradition of Malory,

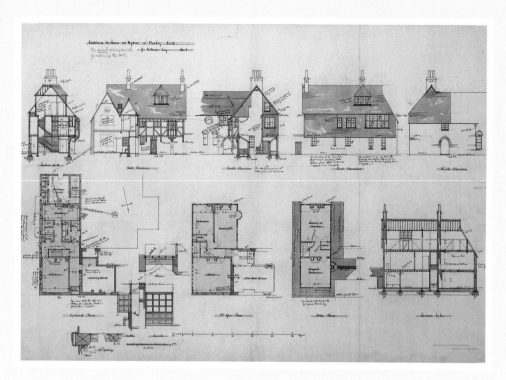

RED HOUSE PLANS (1859)

LEFT: Philip Webb's pen-and-pencil architectural drawings for Red House, without extension.

WILLIAM MORRIS and his friend and architect Philip Webb first discussed the plans for Red House during the summer of 1858 while visiting Gothic churches on holiday together in northern France. Webb's preliminary sketch of a staircase tower, scribbled on the back of a map in a popular guide, is the forerunner of the meticulous pencil, pen, ink, and watercolor architectural drawings for Red House, signed "PHILIP WEBB ARCHT 7 GT ORMOND ST. LONDON," which formed part of the contract with the builder, William Kent, for the construction of the house in 1859.

Red House was Webb's first commission as an independent architect, and his plans specify every detail, together with later penciled alterations, which hint at the close involvement of a fairly demanding client. Indeed, Morris was so keen to oversee the work on the house that he and Jane installed themselves at Aberleigh Lodge, which neighbored the site, so that he could keep a strict eye on the progress of the builders and watch their "Palace of Art" arise amid the orchard of apple trees at Upton, the site they had chosen for its proximity to the newly opened North Kent railway line and the old pilgrims' route to Canterbury.

The feeling in Red House is youthful, artistic, and highly romantic. Light pours in through windows that offer views of Morris's garden planned along compartmentalized medieval lines, with kitchen gardens, orchards, a bowling green, and rose walks for Jane. Generous-sized doors lead from room to room so that each space flows into the next, anticipating open-plan living and making the house "admirable to live in," according to Rossetti, who, with his wife, the lovely Lizzie Siddal, was a frequent visitor in the early days.

Philip Webb, though modest and shy in public, had a fearsome reputation for highmindedness and high standards. Nowadays it is common to hear him called the father figure of the Arts & Crafts Movement. In the 1880s and 1890s he was commissioned to design a number of important country houses, including Clouds in Wiltshire (1886) and Standen in Sussex (1891), both decorated by Morris & Co. A lifelong socialist, he earned less than £320 a year—only slightly more than a master mason—during this period, and after his death in 1915 was likened by his assistant George Jack to sunshine "which pleases and it passes, but it also makes things grow."

Froissart, and later Norse legend and Icelandic sagas. His time at Oxford deepened his fondness for medieval turrets, coiling staircases and graceful spires. Red House gave him an opportunity to realize his dream of a home rich in such fairytale details. It was never grand, but capacious and comfortable, with a hint of fantasy.

The house had four large bedrooms, another tiny one, and a partitioned dormitory for the cook and two maids at the far end of the western wing. Narrow stairs led down from this to the kitchen and scullery, while a magnificent oak staircase with tapered newels guided guests up from the deep expansive entrance hall to the upper rooms, which included the drawing room with its high arched ceiling, ribbed with beams, and the adjacent light-flooded studio, with its views across orchards and the rolling Kent countryside. Here, Morris installed a big settle from his Red Lion Square rooms, which Webb transformed by means of a balustrade around the top into a miniature minstrels' gallery. Webb designed much of the furniture himself in a solid and monumental style, its heaviness

lightened by the medieval scenes painted on it by Morris, Burne-Jones, and Rossetti, the latter of whom was effusive in his enthusiasm for the project, calling it "a most noble work in every way, and more a poem than a house."

The walls of the rooms were white, and the soaring ceilings were decorated with geometric patterns. Elaborate schemes were devised for embroidered panels to decorate the dining room and for frescoes to be painted directly on to the fresh plaster in the drawing room. Burne-Jones painted Morris into a mural, depicting him as medieval king, wearing a deep-blue robe with gold borders, at a crowded wedding feast. Beside him, in a wimple, crowned as queen, is his wife, Jane. Charles Faulkner, who would later become one of the partners in the firm of Morris, Marshall, Faulkner & Co., helped to paint patterns on the walls, and Rossetti filled in the spaces left by Morris. Here, in Red House, life and art merged. Twenty years later, in his lecture series entitled "How we Live and How we Might Live," Morris drew on this time for his definition of true domesticity:

"It is not an original remark, but I make it here, that my home is where I meet people with whom I sympathise, whom I love."

Each weekend Morris and Jane, radiantly happy in the early years of their marriage, would stand in the wide, welcoming porch and greet their friends, leading them into the generously proportioned hall that so suited Morris's big booming personality. Their little daughters, Jenny and May, would duck between the legs of Algernon Charles Swinburne, Rossetti, Madox Brown, and Burne-Jones while Morris descended to his wine cellar, returning with bottles tucked under his arm and a broad smile on his face. For Morris, light, warmth, fellowship, and beauty fostered by decoration was what made a successful "home." It was a recipe he followed in all his houses, including Kelmscott Manor near Lechlade in Gloucestershire, which he rented in 1871 as a country retreat.

The relationship between the house and its setting was a matter of paramount importance to Morris and Webb, and to the succeeding architects of the Arts & Crafts Movement, such as Ernest Prior, M. H. Baillie Scott, Charles Voysey, Ernest Gimson, and Edwin Lutyens, the latter of whom engaged in an important collaboration with Gertrude Jekyll that was to prove pivotal to the whole development of the English garden style. They stressed the need for simplicity, and aimed to design houses that enhanced rather than dominated their surroundings, combining features found in old houses and churches, and in museums, with contemporary design. The importance of integrating the designs of furnishings and buildings was emphasized, and indulgence in ornament for ornament's sake was avoided.

The Movement chose to construct its buildings from indigenous materials and strove above all to build in the local traditions—using stonework in the Cotswolds, pargeted plasterwork in Essex, tile-hanging in Kent, and roughcast in the Lake District—both for economic and aesthetic reasons. It also spearheaded a revival of traditional construction methods, focussing on the details and techniques of crafts such as ornamental plasterwork, ironwork, carving, and sculpture. Some members, like Webb, worked in

collaboration with Morris on the internal decoration, while others recommended his papers, textiles, and furniture to their customers, since a Morris interior perfectly suited the new Arts & Crafts buildings, many of which were small-scale, habitable, and affordable homes for a newly prosperous professional class.

In 1877 Morris wrote to the editor of *The Athenaeum* to express his profound dismay at the destructive effects of a practice that went under the misleading title of "restoration":

> "My eye just now caught the word 'restoration' in the morning paper, and, on looking closer, I saw that this time it is nothing less than the Minster of Tewkesbury that is to be destroyed by Sir Gilbert Scott. Is it altogether too late to do something to save it—it and whatever else beautiful or historical is still left us on the sites of the ancient buildings we were once so famous for?"

ABOVE: In the summer of 1871, William Morris signed a joint lease with Dante Gabriel Rossetti on Kelmscott Manor (a Tudor farmhouse built of local limestone on the edge of the village of Kelmscott in 1570, with an additional wing added to the northeast corner c. 1665). It would become his most beloved home.

OVERLEAF: Kelmscott became Morris's country home. He spoke of it fondly as: "A house that I love with a reasonable love I think . . . so much has the old house grown up out of the soil and lives of those that lived on it."

ABOVE: Standen in West Sussex, designed by Philip Webb for the solicitor James Beale in 1891–4.

LEFT: This charming pavilion, nestled among the massed rhododendrons, provided the Beales and their guests with a shady spot from which to watch a croquet game on the lawn below the southeastern corner of the house.

Morris had found a new crusade and, in 1877, he was instrumental in founding, with Webb and others, the Society for the Protection of Ancient Buildings (SPAB), also known affectionately as "Anti-Scrape." The Society objected to the way in which old buildings were being restored and set itself up as a watchdog body, a prototype pressure group, determined to locate and list all ancient buildings left unrestored in an effort to forestall their unsympathetic alteration. A public circular issued by SPAB urged "the proper care" of monuments:

> "Watch an old building with an anxious care; count its stones as you would jewels of a crown; bind it together where it loosens, stay it with timber where it declines. Do not care about the unsightliness of the aid; better a crutch than a lost limb; and do this tenderly, reverently, continually, and many a generation will still be born to pass away beneath its shadow."

The Society provided a valuable platform for the dissemination of Morris's and Webb's ideas, and helped to form and nurture the architectural ideology of Arts & Crafts proponents like Ernest Gimson, W. R. Lethaby, C. R. Ashbee, Detmar Blow, Alfred Powell, and Ernest and Sidney Barnsley, while preserving many old churches, barns, and vernacular buildings for posterity. However, Morris's attacks upon his old mentor G. E. Street and his *bête noire* George Gilbert Scott lost him friends, and his decision to no longer accept stained glass commissions from churches under restoration lost the firm money.

The Arts & Crafts Movement's emphasis on the importance of harmony and repose extended beyond the houses its architects designed to the immediate surroundings. The inspiration for the ideal Arts & Crafts garden could be found in a rustically romantic old England, crammed with the kind of indigenous plants—old roses, eyebright, fiery nasturtiums, sunflowers, and pinks—immortalized by Morris in his patterns for wallpapers, fabrics, and carpets. There was a move away from the hard-edged geometry of the rigidly planned Victorian garden, with its exotic foreign hothouse flowers—palms and orchids, and the big showy garden shrubs such as rhododendrons and hydrangeas.

The pioneering garden designers William Robinson and Gertrude Jekyll, among others, created a new, fresh style that relied, not on seasonal bedding schemes, but natural groupings and an idealized rural profusion of sweet-smelling flowers such as hollyhocks and wallflowers. This was more manageable for the burgeoning new middle class and better suited their smaller gardens. Robinson wrote, "I believe that the best results can only be got by the owner who knows and loves his ground. The great evil is the stereotyped plan . . ." Passionate and persuasive, Robinson—like William Morris—put his own ideas into practice in the garden of Gravetye Manor, a handsome Elizabethan gabled mansion house, which he bought in 1885 at the age of forty-seven on the proceeds of his highly popular publications, including *The Wild Garden* and *The English Flower Garden*.

For Gertrude Jekyll the purpose of a garden was "to give delight and to give refreshment of mind, to soothe, to refine and to lift up the heart." Trained as a painter at the South Kensington School of Art, she turned to garden design in her forties, as her eyesight began to fail, and collaborated with the much younger Edwin Lutyens on some of the finest gardens in England. She referred to herself as an "artist-gardener" and in *Color Schemes for the Flower Garden* noted that "when the eye is trained to perceive pictorial effect, it is frequently struck by something—some combination of grouping, lighting, and color—that is seen to have that complete aspect of unity and beauty that to the artist's eye forms a picture."

RIGHT: Gravetye Manor—exceptionally situated in the rolling countryside of West Sussex —was where, over a period of fifty years, William Robinson created his garden, famous for natural planting and profuse mixed groupings. He held strong views and was not interested in discoursing in Latin, insisting that every plant should have an English name.

CHAPTER TWO

DESIGNS FOR LIVING

THE INTERIOR

LEFT: The restored drawing room at Standen has lighting fixtures by Webb and Benson, Morris's "Tulip and Rose" woven wool hangings, a particularly fine example of a hand-knotted Merton Abbey carpet (designed by John Henry Dearle), and Morris's "Sunflower" wallpaper and, though empty, seems to await the arrival of the Beale family, stylishly dressed for dinner.

ABOVE RIGHT: William Morris, photographed c. 1870.

"All rooms ought to look as if they were lived in, and to have, so to say, a friendly welcome ready for the incomer."

WILLIAM MORRIS, "MAKING THE BEST OF IT," 1880

LEFT: One of Morris's earliest wallpaper designs—"Trellis" (1862).

RIGHT: The oak staircase in the hall at Red House, showing part of the ceiling painted in bold geometric patterns.

FAR RIGHT: The ample hall of Red House and the open door, where Janey and Morris would stand together to welcome their many guests.

A WILLIAM MORRIS INTERIOR blends the homely with the heroic, the practical with the romantic, simplicity with beauty. While Morris's interiors appear comfortable to the modern eye, they seemed shockingly stark to his Victorian contemporaries, brought up in an age of conspicuous consumption to parade their wealth and taste by surrounding themselves with more and more emblems of it. The fashionable Victorian living room was a riot of different styles—Classical, Moorish, and mock-Tudor—stuffed with *objects d'art*, crammed with furniture, festooned, fringed, and tasseled, and horizontally banded and bordered with dizzying patterns from skirting board to dado, to cornice and ceiling, all treated differently.

Morris believed that the accumulation of useless things had dulled the public's capacity to appreciate and value beauty and—in a lesson that we might well profit from today—lectured against the acquisitiveness of the fortunate classes, referring to them, scathingly, as "digesting machines." "Believe me," he warned, "if we want art to begin at home as it must, we must clear our houses of troublesome superfluities that are for ever in our way." With characteristic forthrightness, he declared, "I have never been in any rich man's home which would not have looked the better for having a bonfire made outside it of nine-tenths of all it held."

In his 1880 lecture "Making the Best of It," Morris asserted that "no room of the richest man should look grand enough to make a

simple man shrink in it, or luxurious enough to make a thoughtful man feel ashamed in it; it will not do so if Art be at home there, for she has no foes so deadly as insolence and waste." He always applied this philosophy to his own homes, and when George Bernard Shaw first visited him at his Hammersmith address, he was immediately struck by the daring absence of tablecloths and the way Morris had suspended a Persian carpet "so lovely that it would have been a sin to walk on it . . . halfway across the ceiling." Shaw saw at once that for Morris the table was "itself an ornament and not a clothes horse," though he admitted this was "an innovation so staggering" as to be quite simply years ahead of its time.

Morris's first response to his own surroundings—from the bachelor rooms at 17 Red Lion Square that he shared with Burne-Jones to the six homes he lived in over the years with Jane and his two daughters—was to put his own stamp on them. He was an innovative interior designer, championing a return to simplicity and sincerity, through the application of quality materials, rich and

suggestive surface decoration, and sound workmanship. Morris actualized his ideas and schemes in his own homes, where the drawing room was usually his most dramatic set-piece, and each served as an advertisement for the firm.

The medieval mood of Red House was recreated in a number of Morris's grander, more lavish commissions, but at 26 Queen Square and his two Kelmscotts a new preference for comfort and simplicity had begun to emerge. The firm's manager George Wardle recalled the Queen Square rooms as "extremely simple, very beautiful." Morris had done his best to conquer "the dinginess of the neighbourhood" by making the house shine with whitewash, "a background that," according to Georgiana Burne-Jones, a regular at the Morris's weekly dinners, "shewed better than any other the beautiful fabrics with which the house was furnished."

Morris's daughters, Jenny and May, were probably too young to miss the large garden at Red House—echoed in the cheerful "Trellis" wallpaper in their Queen Square nursery—but Jane, who had

enjoyed five years as chatelaine of her own medievally inspired country house, was disappointed by the move back to Bloomsbury, where she was living "above the shop," and responded by lapsing into silence and, in the manner of the time, taking increasingly to her sofa, in the grip of a mysterious languor. The old Red House merriment was gone.

Jane's strange, haunting beauty and semi-invalid status reignited the interest of Dante Gabriel Rossetti, and she began to pose for him at his house in Cheyne Walk. Soon gossip began to circulate about "Gabriel being so fond of Mrs. Top." Morris's response to the deepening relationship between his wife and one of his best friends and business partners was extraordinarily forbearing. In the most conventional of times, he took the unconventional course of finding a secluded house in the country, where the couple could spend the long summer months together. He found Kelmscott Manor advertised in a house agent's catalog and went to inspect it twice before signing, with Rossetti, a joint

tenancy lease in 1871. "We have taken a little place deep down in the country," he wrote to Georgiana Burne-Jones, "a beautiful and strangely naïf house, Elizabethan in appearance . . . within a stone's throw of the baby Thames, in the most beautiful grey little hamlet called Kelmscott."

As tenants, they did little to the structure of the house beyond repairing rotten floorboards but, naturally enough, they began work at once on the interior, decorating the rooms with fabrics and tiles ordered from the firm. The big parlor had "some pleasing George I panelling" that Jane repainted white, providing a simple background for comfortable chairs covered in Morris's own "Peacock and Dragon" design. The house, she wrote to Philip Webb was, "all delightful and home-like to me and I love it."

Jane and Rossetti behaved with some discretion at Kelmscott that first summer. Jane had her own bedroom: a cool, clean, west-facing room with a four-poster bed and a seventeenth-century chest of drawers, on which she placed the lovely jewel casket that

LEFT AND ABOVE: Three views of Jane Morris's west-facing "Willow" papered bedroom at Kelmscott Manor, showing the jewel casket made by Rossetti and Lizzie Siddal as a gift for Jane. The chintz hangings on the mahogany four-poster bed are also made up in the "Willow" pattern. The oil painting of Jane Morris is a copy made by Charles Fairfax Murray in 1893 of Rossetti's "Water-willow" portrait, painted in 1871 during that first idyllic summer at Kelmscott.

Lizzie Siddal and Rossetti had painted for her as a wedding present. Rossetti moved into the "tapestry room."

During the height of his wife's affair, Morris spent a good deal of time traveling to Iceland, and simply working. However, after Rossetti's breakdown—provoked by savage criticism of his poems and his morals—and the painful unraveling of his business partnership, he felt able to spend more time in the place May Morris and her sister Jenny considered "the only house in England worth inhabiting."

As evidence of his attachment to his Oxfordshire "haunt of ancient peace," in 1878 Morris renamed his new Hammersmith home "Kelmscott House." The new house was in a poor state of repair but had huge potential and "could easily be done up at a cost of money" and "made very beautiful with a touch of my art," reasoned Morris, when Jane mentioned the damp basement and the "frightful" kitchen.

Morris's daughters, May and Jenny, "as loyal worshippers in the home circle," considered the newly decorated Kelmscott House drawing room to be not "one of the prettiest rooms in London, but just *the* most beautiful." It was a superb room, thirty-seven feet long, running the width of the house on the first floor, with five tall windows commanding wide views of the River Thames. Morris installed the massive pillared grate that Philip Webb had designed for Queen Square and draped the walls, from floor to picture rail, with his double-woven woollen "Bird" fabric, arranged in folds. The predominantly blue effect was enhanced by a simple blue

carpet that acted as a neutral background to the glowing colors of the oriental rugs. The room was furnished with his own "Morris" adjustable chairs and a high curved-back settle by Philip Webb, painted with sunflowers, which faced the wardrobe adorned with scenes from Chaucer's *The Prioress's Tale* that had been a joint wedding present from Burne-Jones and Philip Webb. Morris's collection of William De Morgan lusterware stood along the overmantel, and "the discreet glimmer of old glass" could be glimpsed in recessed cupboards at the far end of the room, which displayed his collection of antique opalescent glass. May called it a "haven of peace and sweet colour, breathing harmony and simplicity."

Morris leased the house in 1878 and, at a time when his annual income was around £1,200, spent over £1,000 on the redecoration. It was in this house that many of his ideas and principles of interior design were hammered out to produce a series of lectures on the subject, entitled "Hopes and Fears for Art" (1878–81). Despite being a fluent writer of verse, novels, and letters, Morris found the preparation for his lectures grueling. "I know what I want to say," he wrote to Georgiana Burne-Jones, "but the cursed words go to water between my fingers." However, Morris need not have worried. His direct approach made him much in demand as a speaker, and the relaxed, conversational tone of the lectures made them popular in print as well.

Honesty is at the heart of Morris's approach to interior decoration. "Don't think too much of style," he urged his audience

TRELLIS WALLPAPER DESIGN (1862)

RED HOUSE was a living manifesto of Morris's philosophy and a laboratory for his ideas. It was there that he first experimented with wallpaper designs, producing "Trellis," "Daisy," and "Fruit"—his first commercial designs—in 1862. "Trellis" was directly inspired by the medieval garden he had created around the well court at the back of Red House, which featured "wattled rose-trellises inclosing richly-flowered square garden plots."

The wild rose had long been a special favorite with Morris, who declared that "nothing can be more beautiful than a wayside bush of it, nor can any scent be as sweet and pure as its scent." So we should not be especially surprised that he chose it for a starring role in his first paper. He turned to his friend Philip Webb, however, for the birds. Webb produced a charming watercolor study, which Morris incorporated into the final design. Technical difficulties were responsible for the fifteen-month delay between Morris completing the layout and officially registering the design in February 1864. He had hoped to print the papers himself using oil colors and etched zinc plates, but this proved impossible and he handed the production over to Jeffrey & Co., who employed the standard woodblock process and distemper colors.

The design was far from being a wild or immediate success, however. Warington Taylor, the firm's manager, referred to the "limited sale of our papers" in a letter to Webb and in the end Morris had to rely on personal contacts and recommendations. Rossetti persuaded his patron, Frederick Leyland, a northern shipping magnate, to use "Trellis" (and "Daisy" and "Fruit") at Speke Hall, his house near Liverpool in 1867.

Morris remained fond of the pattern and used it in the girls' nursery when the family moved from Red House to Queen Square in 1865, and he hung a blue-ground version of "Trellis" in his bedroom at Kelmscott House, ten years after first conceiving the design. It was also adapted for embroidered bed-hangings, executed by Lily Yeats, Maude Deacon, Ellen Wright, and May Morris between 1891 and 1894, which can be seen at Kelmscott Manor, and can be viewed on the walls of the lobby at Standen.

LEFT: A detail of one of the three easy chairs, upholstered in "Peacock and Dragon" woven wool, which make a group around the fireplace in the Panelled Room at Kelmscott Manor.

RIGHT: The Green Room at Kelmscott Manor, showing the "Kennet" chintz, designed by Morris in 1883. The tiles in the fireplace are all Morris designs. The seventeenth-century oak chair with book-box in the seat was always known as Jenny's chair.

in 1881, stressing instead a positive enjoyment of plain surfaces, natural textures, and simple forms, enriched by pure color and bold patterns. He drew extensively on his notions of an idealized medieval past, striving to break down the boundaries between art and craftsmanship, and stressed the need to restore dignity to the worker robbed of any satisfaction in his labors by the steamroller of the industrial revolution. In a lecture entitled "Art and the Beauty of the Earth" in 1881, Morris explained:

> "In almost all cases there is no sympathy between the designer and the man who carries out the design . . . I know by experience that the making of design after design—mere diagrams, mind you—without oneself executing them, is a great strain upon the mind. It is necessary, unless all workmen of all grades are to be permanently degraded into machines, that the hand should rest the mind as well as the mind the hand. And I say that this is the kind of work which the world has lost, supplying its place with the work which is the result of the division of labour."

In his lecture "The Beauty of Life" (1880), presented to an audience assembled at the Birmingham School of Art and Design,

Morris described the contents of his ideal room, in which "the wall itself must be ornamented with some beautiful and restful pattern." He insisted that, "Simplicity of life, even the barest, is not a misery, but the very foundation of refinement," adding "this simplicity you may make as costly as you please or can . . . and you may hang your walls with tapestry instead of whitewash or paper; or you may cover them with mosaic, or have them frescoed by a great painter: all this is not luxury, if it be done for beauty's sake, and not for show." Summarizing his views on the hazards of clutter in the home, he urged,

> "Believe me, if we want art to begin at home, as it must, we must clear our houses of troublesome superfluities that are for ever in our way: conventional comforts that are no real comforts, and do but make work for servants and doctors: if you want a golden rule that will fit everybody, this is it: 'Have nothing in your houses that you do not know to be useful or believe to be beautiful.'"

Morris's famous maxim is as valid today as when he first uttered it in 1880, and his ideas had a huge, reverberating impact. Mrs. Earle, a best-selling Victorian author, recalled the "revelation" of her first visit to Morris's Queen Square showroom:

"It had the effect of a sudden opening of a window in a dark room. All was revealed — the beauty of simplicity, the usefulness of form, the fascination of design and the charm of delicate colour. Added to this came the appreciation of the things that had gone before, and which in my time had been hidden away. I came back to the various houses to which I had been accustomed with a sigh of despair; but the first step towards progress must always be discontent with what one has and with one's own ignorance."

Thus Morris & Co. simultaneously shaped and supplied the tastes of a burgeoning middle-class, which eagerly embraced the simple elegance, rich colors, liquid lines, and naturalistic inspiration of the Morris "look" and implemented it in their Arts-&-Crafts-inspired homes in the new districts of Bedford Park and Hampstead Garden Suburb. No fashionable home was without some item from the Oxford Street showrooms of Morris & Co., and to secure the services of Morris himself was considered quite a coup. "[George] Wardle is doing most of the house," confided Walter Bagehot, a lawyer, who had commissioned the firm to decorate his London house in Queen's Gate Place, "but the great man himself, William Morris, is composing the drawing room, as he would an ode."

Following Morris's restructuring of the business with himself as sole proprietor, he began to attract a new type of client, the sort of wealthy buyer who had patronized the Pre-Raphaelite painters, manufacturers, and merchants. Among these clients were Sir Lowthian Bell, a northern industrialist; William Knox D'Arcy, a mining engineer; and Alexander Ionides, a Greek importer and patron of the arts, whose Holland Park house was praised in *The Studio* magazine for its "consistent example of the use of fabrics and patterns designed chiefly by Mr. Morris" and

RIGHT: The romance and drama of the singular upstairs Tapestry Room at Kelmscott Manor appealed hugely to Dante Gabriel Rossetti, who claimed it for his studio, though after his departure it became a room much more closely associated with Morris.

BULLERSWOOD CARPET (1889)

HAND-KNOTTED WITH WOOLLEN PILE ON A COTTON WARP, 764.8 x 398.8 CM

WILLIAM MORRIS cherished fond memories of his early experiments at carpet weaving in the coach house and adjoining stable at Kelmscott House, Hammersmith, in the late 1870s. There he began production of his distinctive, if prohibitively expensive, hand-knotted "Hammersmith" carpets, which carried the identifying mark in the border, composed of a hammer, a capital "M" and stylized waves. Soon, however, the coach house proved too cramped to work in comfort, and so, in 1881, the operation was moved to Merton Abbey, where larger looms had been installed and there was space, on fine days, for Morris to spread the finished carpets on the lawn so that he might see them "all at once" rather than "piecemeal." It was here that the "Bullerswood" carpet—one of Morris's more spectacular and elaborate designs—was made for the Sandersons—family friends, with whom Jane Morris had traveled abroad on at least one occasion. John Sanderson, a successful wool merchant, commissioned Morris & Co. to refurbish Bullerswood, his house in Chislehurst, Kent, in 1889. Originally built in 1866, it had recently been extended by Ernest Newton for the expanding family (there were nine Sanderson children), and it seems that William Morris was eager to supervise the project in person. Two Hammersmith carpets were ordered for the house—one for the hall and the other for the drawing room which, according to Victoria and Albert Museum records dating from a visit to the house in 1921, was "decorated by William Morris under his personal supervision and nothing was allowed to be placed in it in addition to the objects executed by himself." This would strongly suggest that the Bullerswood carpet—which was was exhibited at the Arts & Crafts Exhibition in 1893—was the work of Morris alone, though recently it has been suggested that the bold, monumental design shows the strong influence of John Henry Dearle and may therefore have been a collaborative project. Three versions are known to have been made. The Victoria and Albert Museum have one, another is on loan to Kelmscott Manor, and the third is thought to be in Australia.

RIGHT: The "Honeysuckle Room" at Wightwick Manor (1887–93) in the West Midlands, so called because of Morris's printed linen "Honeysuckle," which has been in the house since it was built. The chairs are from Morris & Co., as is the carpet, which William Morris designed himself.

heralded as "the first flower of the 'Movement' in aesthetic furnishing." Another important client was the aristocratic Howard family, with whom Morris enjoyed a long association, lavishing ten years on the decoration of their London house at Palace Green and putting himself out equally for Naworth Castle and Castle Howard, which were decorated with carpets, tapestries, and textiles supplied by Morris & Co.

These immensely wealthy customers commissioned the firm to redecorate entire houses in London and the country, which were featured under headings such as "An Epoch-Making House" or "A Kensington Interior" in influential magazines such as *Country Life, The Art Journal* and *The Studio*, further promoting and popularizing Morris's ideas. The Morris message reached continental Europe through the pages of *Der Moderne Stil* and Hermann Muthesius's influential *Das Englische Haus*; in the United States, Gustav Stickley devoted the first issue of his important new publication *The Craftsman* to John Ruskin and the second

to William Morris, whom he hailed as "a household name throughout America."

A number of houses decorated by the firm are open to the public, including Standen in East Sussex, which the prosperous solicitor James Beale commissioned from Philip Webb in 1891 as a weekend home for his family, and Wightwick Manor, near Wolverhampton, the romantic mock-Elizabethan home of Theodore Mander, a successful paint and varnish manufacturer, which boasts a great many Morris textiles. Webb designed the interior of Standen with particular care and created light-filled, plain, paneled rooms, enlivened by the color and pattern of his great friend William Morris's wallpapers and fabrics.

One of the last commissions Morris supervised himself was the interior decoration of Bullerswood, the Kent home of the Sanderson family, for which he created a beautiful Hammersmith carpet, featuring a bird motif known as "Bullerswood," which was laid in the plain white-walled drawing room. No wallpapers were

used at all in the ground-floor rooms, which Morris kept white with patternwork on cornices and ceilings, though they did make an appearance in the bedrooms, one of which had "walls hung with a sort of Arras, designed and printed by Morris," according to an inventory made in 1921 when the contents of the house were sold.

In the 1880s politics occupied more of Morris's time, and he began to delegate even large decorative schemes such as the one for Stanmore Hall in Middlesex—the country home of the fabulously wealthy mining magnate William Knox D'Arcy—to his assistant John Henry Dearle, himself a talented designer, who became Art Director of the firm after Morris's death, in 1896. Dearle produced original designs for the carpets and textiles in Stanmore Hall, along with painted decoration for the walls and ceilings, and the result is more lavish than it might have been had Morris completed it himself. The "Holy Grail" tapestries designed by Burne-Jones, Morris, and Dearle for the dining room were

ABOVE AND RIGHT:
A detail of one of the elaborate ceilings at Wightwick Manor (above) is complemented by a closeup view of that of the Old Debating Chamber (now the library) of the Oxford Union Society (right), which Morris, Rossetti, Burne-Jones, and others decorated in their "jovial campaign" of 1857.

probably the most ambitious ever made by Morris & Co., and a number of pieces of furniture were specially made by the firm, including an inlaid bureau designed by George Jack. "Messrs William Morris & Co. have had a free hand, not merely in such matters as usually fall within the scope of decorators, but in the hangings, furniture and carpets," reported the *The Studio,* going on rhapsodically to praise the splendor of the rooms and the "sumptuous decoration kept within proper proportion."

Morris had great feeling for interflowing spaces, and many of his design schemes anticipate the open and airy interiors popular today. "The house that would please me," he commented to W. B. Yeats, "would be some great room where one talked to one's friends in one corner, and ate in another, and slept in another and worked in another." In his own time his ideas were enthusiastically embraced and adapted by the Arts & Crafts Movement, pointing the way to lighter, brighter, more functional interiors that encouraged a

more rational use of space. In the United States, Gustav Stickley, Morris's spiritual heir, promoted the ideal family home in his magazine *The Craftsman,* identifying the living room as "a place where work is to be done . . . the haven of rest . . . the place where children grow and thrive," and recommending a determinedly simple design scheme of plain walls with a deep frieze of stylized trees, a leather armchair, a wood-framed settle, a circular side table, and plain, unlined curtains at the windows. "It is here," he insisted, "that we should be our best."

For Morris, the choice of pattern depended on the character of the room. He did away with dadoes altogether, or painted the woodwork below the rail white, and popularized a more harmonious effect, achieved by keeping the walls simple, either painted with a plain color (or often white, "the perfect foil to most colors") or covered with wallpaper, draped with printed cotton or woven damask. If the woodwork was particularly attractive, he might leave it unstained or varnished, and let the pattern on the

ABOVE: The White Drawing Room at Blackwell in Cumbria—designed by M. H. Baillie-Scott as a holiday home for Edward Holt, Lord Mayor of Manchester—incorporates his trademark inglenook, and is considered to be one of his best interiors.

carpet, chairs, and sofas make the main statement. "Covers need not be uniform," he wrote encouragingly, "they may be of two or three or four kinds, according to the size of the room and the number of pieces."

Morris aimed for comfort and an aura of relaxation. A typical drawing room decorated by the firm would include a number of upholstered chairs and sofas, perhaps a settle by the tiled fireplace, cabinets along the walls, and several tables. Added points of color would be provided by the glowing embroidered cushion covers on rush-seated chairs from Morris's highly popular "Sussex" range, which would be placed around the room, and a high wooden mantelpiece would provide a shelf for lusterware. The wooden planked floor would be covered with rugs and rectangular "Hammersmith" carpets. The different patterns in each individual aspect of the scheme would be unified by the readily identifiable "Morris" style, the simple elegance of which still looks fresh and modern more than a century later.

CHAPTER THREE

DECORATIVE PATTERNS

WALLPAPERS AND WOVEN FABRICS

LEFT: The corner of the billiard room at Wightwick Manor, which amply demonstrates the "layered" effect of the Morris look, with "Bird" pattern tapestry weave curtains, "Pimpernel" wallpaper, and a Kidderminster carpet in "Lily" design of 1877. The seat is covered in "Tulip and Rose" woven fabric.

ABOVE RIGHT: Morris may be older in this picture, but he stares out at the world with the steady fervent gaze of one with a message to communicate.

"Ornamental pattern work, to be raised above the contempt of reasonable men, must possess three qualities: beauty, imagination and order."

WILLIAM MORRIS, "SOME HINTS ON PATTERN DESIGNING," 1881

WILLIAM MORRIS IS best known to us today for his distinctive, and seemingly timeless, wallpapers. Indeed, his first three designs— "Daisy," "Fruit," and "Trellis"—can still be purchased almost 150 years after he first created them. Back in 1862, which was a boom time for the wallpaper industry, there was nothing quite like them. The prevailing Victorian taste favored the florid "French" styles of the early 1850s or the "Reformist" style popularized by Augustus Pugin, whose diamond, or diaper, motif appeared most famously on his wallpaper designs for the Houses of Parliament. From the 1840s, new techniques for mass production had revolutionized the decoration of interior walls, which had usually been painted, sometimes marbled or grained, to look like wood, or stenciled and enlivened with a decorative border. Fabrics such as watered silk or printed damask had been popular wall coverings for wealthier homes, but once rolls of high-quality wallpaper began to be commercially produced by firms such as Jeffrey & Co., they were soon seen on the walls of most Victorian homes.

By the time Morris entered the market, technological advances had pushed production up to nineteen million rolls per annum. Given the prominent part wallpaper has played in the public perception of Morris both in his own lifetime—Henry James called him "the poet and paper-maker"—and today, his claim that "printing patterns on paper for wall hangings" was only a "quite modern and very humble, but, as things go, useful art" seems remarkably understated.

Morris's choice of Jeffrey & Co. as printers proved shrewd and profitable for all concerned. The company was already printing Owen Jones's influential patterns—including a series of elaborate papers designed by Jones for the Viceroy's Palace in Cairo—and had an established reputation as manufacturers of high-quality wall decorations. Morris may have seen their stand at the International Exhibition of 1862, when Morris, Marshall, Faulkner & Co. showed there. Always a perfectionistic, exacting client, even he found that Jeffrey & Co. handled his orders "so carefully and with such anxious desire to satisfy" that he willingly subcontracted new designs to them over a long period and established an excellent working relationship with the entrepreneurial Metford Warner, whose flair and innovation put Jeffrey & Co. in the forefront of "artistic" production. Walter Crane designed papers for Jeffrey & Co., along with E. W. Godwin, William Burges, Albert Moore, and Charles Eastlake. Crane referred to Warner as "a man of taste and judgement," who spared "no pains to get the proper effect of a pattern."

As ever, Morris was establishing the market rather than just supplying it, and revolutionizing the tastes of his own time. His flat, rhythmical hand-printed patterns, based on medieval motifs and on nature, were strikingly fresh and original. Walter Crane, writing in *Scribers Magazine*, applauded the way his papers "acknowledged the wall" and expressed the proportions of the room, instead of trying to hide both "under bunches of sketchy roses and vertical stripes." His astonishingly fertile imagination found inspiration in the native British hedgerows, and the flowers and fruits growing in his garden at Red House (and later from the wildflowers, willow-bordered river, and water meadows around Kelmscott Manor, which provided the inspiration for his long-leafed, and most enduringly popular "Willow" design).

By celebrating simple English flowers such as the daisy, honeysuckle, sunflower, and eyebright, Morris moved away from overpowering formal patterns based on the exotic hothouse flowers so favored by the Victorians. In a lecture entitled "Some Hints on Pattern Designing" (1881), he explained that, "Wallpapers must operate within

a little depth. There must be a slight illusion—not as to the forms of the motif, but as to relative depth." He demonstrates this in "Daisy", for example, where the pattern is pleasantly balanced and clearly ornamental, with no recession and no imitation of accidental details, and in his 1884 design "Wild Tulip," which was, for May Morris "all Kelmscott" because "the peony and wild tulip are two of the richest blossomings of the spring garden at the Manor."

Between 1862 and 1896 the firm produced a wide range of sweeping, naturalistic patterns for wallpapers and fabrics in warm, subtle colors. The prices of the wallpapers varied, from the least expensive machine prints to hand-printed papers, and much more expensive, elaborate gold-ground paper. Many of the hand-printed papers—such as "Daisy" and "Fruit," which was also known as "Pomegranate"—came with a choice of light, medium, or dark background colors.

These naturalistic wallpaper designs by Morris proved immensely popular with the public. The *Punch* cartoonist Linley Sambourne, who along with his colleague George du Maurier took pot shots at

Morris, Rossetti, and Burne-Jones, nevertheless bought Morris's wallpapers and much else besides from Morris & Co.; "Fruit" wallpaper decorated the hallway, and morning and dining rooms of his Stafford Terrace house. Margaret Beale ordered all the wallpapers, and a fair number of chintzes for hangings and curtains, for Standen from Morris & Co., hanging "Fruit" in the billiard room, "Sunflower" in the drawing room and "Trellis," "Larkspur," "Willow," and "Bachelor's Button" elsewhere in the house. By 1882, one author noted that Morris's wallpapers had been eagerly pasted on to the walls of the majority of the houses on Richard Norman Shaw's Bedford Park estate by their artistic occupants.

The success of the firm was further boosted by a new vogue for interior decoration prompted by the publication of Charles Eastlake's influential *Hints on Household Taste* (1868), which promoted the cultivation of a single, cohesive style in the home and paved the way for the Arts & Crafts Movement. The impact of the book was felt in Great Britain, and in the United States, where it

became a bestseller, published in seven editions. Eastlake popularized the decorative scheme that divided the wall into three horizontal sections: a frieze, wallpaper above the dado line, and a darker treatment to the areas subject to wear and tear below. However, Morris considered this to be too much for all but the loftiest rooms. "Never stoop to the ignominy of the paper dado," he warned in his 1880 lecture "Making the Best of It."

Morris frequently addressed the subject of pattern design in his lectures and published works. In a lecture entitled "Textiles, Arts and Crafts" (1888), he advised:

> "Do not be afraid of large patterns, if properly designed they are more restful to the eye than small ones: on the whole, a pattern where the structure is large and the details much broken up is the most useful . . . very small rooms, as well as very large ones, look better ornamented with large patterns."

He cautioned, however, against using more than one pattern of wallpaper in a single room and personally disliked papered ceilings, stating that "a room papered all over would be like a box to live in."

Despite his genius for pattern design, Morris used wallpaper sparingly in his own homes and often opted for a simple whitewash treatment—"on which sun and shadow play so pleasantly"—as a backdrop to the patterns used elsewhere on the carpets, furniture, and embroidered hangings. In a piece of advice that is still useful today, he wrote, "White is perfectly neutral; it is a perfect foil to most colours, and by judicious toning may be assimilated with any. It is therefore manageable without great art." In place of wallpaper Morris would sometimes cover a single wall from the picture rail to the skirting board with one of his own printed cottons, either draped or soft-pleated. This was not, however, a widely copied idea. "People dressed themselves in his wallhangings, covered books with them," commented Morris's first biographer, J. W. Mackail, "but hang walls with them they would not."

LEFT: The study at I Holland Park, the home of Alexander Ionides, showing *The Forest* tapestry (1887). Other textiles and carpets are by Morris.

RIGHT: *Mrs William Morris in a Blue Silk Dress* by Dante Gabriel Rossetti. "When she came into a room in her strangely beautiful garments, looking at least eight feet high, the effect was as if she had walked out of an Egyptian tomb at Luxor," wrote George Bernard Shaw of Janey Morris.

Morris used his own "boldly circular" "Pimpernel" pattern in this way in the classically proportioned dining room of his Hammersmith home, Kelmscott House, lightening the effect by fitting the entire wall facing the window with a white-painted dresser that housed his collection of blue-and-white china and pewter plates. A plain scrubbed oak dining table, surrounded by antique carved oak chairs, dominated the great bowed window, and Rossetti's portrait of *Mrs. William Morris in a Blue Silk Dress* (1868) hung above the Adam mantelpiece. Walter Sickert's sister Helena paid a visit and professed herself impressed by the "deliciously homely" atmosphere and the "exquisite cleanliness of the whole house."

A much more ambitious scheme was implemented at 1 Palace Green, designed by Philip Webb for one of Morris's most important patrons, George Howard, later ninth Earl of Carlisle. It was decorated by the firm over a ten-year period, from 1872 to 1882. The wood-paneled dining room was the set-piece and site of a

magnificent decorative frieze, begun by Burne-Jones and completed by Walter Crane, depicting the myth of Cupid and Psyche. The firm also supplied textiles, tapestries, carpets, and stained glass—many pieces specially designed—for the Howards' London home, and their country houses, Castle Howard, in Yorkshire, and Naworth Castle, near Carlisle.

By the 1870s Morris had become a public figure—albeit at times a controversial one—which proved good for business, and one commission often led to the next or sprang from his close collaboration with Philip Webb. Margaret Beale, for example, lived across the road from the Greek financier Alexander Ionides, who in 1880 commissioned Morris & Co. to entirely redecorate his Holland Park house. Morris took personal control of the work, which gave the entire decorative scheme a real coherence and charm, and the work went on for a period of over eight years. Lewis F. Day, writing in *The Art Journal*, described the house as "full of beautiful things, an ideal interior in its way," though he goes on to note that:

RIGHT: The Willow bedroom at Standen was used for many years by Margaret Beale as her embroidery studio.

"It is far from fulfilling Mr. Morris's ideal of 'Art for the People, by the People', and it is a strange inconsistency in the workings of fate that he, and some of those who think with him, should be so largely engaged in an art which essentially is and must always be for the very few who have the taste to appreciate it, and the purse to pay for it."

Margaret Beale—who had the taste and the purse—would have watched the large Hammersmith carpets, embroidered curtains, table-covers, and re-upholstered chairs being delivered and, on visits, seen the marvelous effect of these things against the background of Morris papered walls. When it came to decorating Standen, she knew exactly where to go.

In 1877 Morris & Co. opened their Oxford Street showroom, enabling a wider public to appreciate the way in which the full range of the firm's goods could "be seen together in such a way that one can support the other . . . and so give a true idea of the decoration that we recommend." Customers could look through sample books of all the textile and wallpaper patterns, or borrow a smaller "table book" to take home and peruse at their leisure. The shop sold small items such as photograph frames, embroidered bellpulls, bags, and cushions, and it excited much interest, though not always from Morris, who wrote thanking Thomas Wardle for his "good wishes

about the shop," adding: "I think it will answer though I can't say I am much excited about it, as I should be if it were a shed with half a dozen looms in it."

Having larger premises in such a fashionable shopping district, however, definitely raised the profile of the firm still higher, and advice on how to implement the firm's style and principles was set out in a brochure:

> "When all is done, the result must be colour, not colours. If there are curtains or carpet or other finishings to be worked up to, you must consider which of them, if any, shall be the predominant colour of the room, and which the subordinate or auxiliary colour. The walls and wood-work have generally the predominating colour, and the carpet the secondary. The curtains will then either blend with the walls, and help to surround the carpet with

a frame of colour contrasting with it . . . or the curtains may be used to harmonise the carpet with the walls. The choice must depend upon the choice of room and the point of departure. . . Contrasting colour, if strong, must be kept within small quantities; if pale or grey, it may be more freely used.

> If the chief colour be red, it will be desirable to have a large area of white for rest to the eye. Blues, grey, green and lighter tints of red should be the variants. Contrast with it should be generally avoided; it wants rather quiet than excitement. Whenever white paint may be used for wood-work, choose it in preference to any other. . ."

The brochure alternately flatters and advises the reader newly interested in color "since house-decoration has begun to interest educated people." Relations with customers were very important

LEFT: "Acanthus," designed by William Morris in 1875, marked the beginning of his move toward large-scale, richly colored, hand-printed wallpapers. It required thirty wood blocks to complete the pattern, making it expensive, at 16 shillings a roll.

to the firm, and commissions such as 1 Palace Green and 1 Holland Park gave them access to other fashionable clients in the wealthier parts of London, such as Mayfair, Belgravia, Kensington, and Knightsbridge.

Most of the firm's work was concentrated in London, but there were also important commissions that required Morris to travel up and down the country. The grand scheme for another Webb house—Rounton Grange, the home of Sir Isaac Lowthian Bell— took Morris to Northallerton, in Yorkshire. For this project, Morris and Burne-Jones designed a set of embroideries on the theme of the "Romaunt of the Rose," to be hung above the painted wooden wainscot in the dining room. These were produced by Margaret Bell and her daughters, Ada and Florence. May Morris recorded how the room was "further enriched with a painted ceiling and Hammersmith carpet." Ada and her brother Hugh became important clients of the firm when they set up their own homes at Smeaton Manor (another Webb/Morris collaboration) and Red

Barns, Coatham, near Redcar, both of which were furnished with embroideries, wall-hangings, upholstery fabrics, and tiles from Morris & Co.

As Morris matured, his wallpaper designs evolved from the relatively naive and simple "Daisy," which was a popular best-seller for Morris & Co., to the more sophisticated and orchestrated patterns of "Larkspur," "Willow," "Acanthus," and "Jasmine" (a complex pattern used by Edward Burne-Jones in the drawing room at The Grange, his home in Fulham). In 1883 the firm produced a brochure to accompany their exhibit at the Foreign Fair in Boston, and in it Morris set out at length his philosophy: "In the Decorative Arts nothing is finally successful which does not satisfy the mind as well as the eye. A pattern may have beautiful parts and be good in certain relations; but, unless it is suitable for the purpose assigned, it will not be a decoration." Morris held firm views on how his customers should select their wallpaper and advised:

"LARKSPUR" WALLPAPER DESIGN (c. 1875)

LEFT: A sample of Morris's "Larkspur" design.

WILLIAM MORRIS bristled with good advice when it came to home decoration: "Whatever you have in your rooms," he advocated in "The Lesser Arts of Life," "think first of the walls, for they are that which makes your house and home."

Morris considered his lovely "Larkspur" wallpaper—with its stylized, frontal flowers and breezy irises, swept up in a lightly meandering trail of foliage—to be one of his more "positive" patterns, not to be used "if there is a reason for keeping the wall very quiet." Instead, he recommended it for rooms with "very low and long" walls, explaining that its "columnar" properties would create a bower effect, breaking up the expanse of wall.

The design belongs to a rich four-year period between 1872 and 1876, during which he produced seventeen new wallpaper patterns, drawing on gardens, orchards, and the British countryside for his inspiration.

"Larkspur" was hand-printed for the firm by Messrs. Jeffrey & Co. of Islington. First, the design was cut on to pear-wood blocks, which were then inked and used for printing the papers. Each color had to be printed separately, making

it a lengthy and laborious business, especially when compared to machine-printing. Morris supervised the process carefully, from the cutting of the blocks to the mixing of the distemper, and Metford Warner, the proprietor of Jeffrey & Co., remembered him as an exacting client who, on one occasion set aside an entire set of expensive blocks because he was not satisfied with the design.

The wallpaper log books kept by Jeffrey & Co. present a glowing collage of Morris papers, with small samples pasted into old account books, annotated in the margins with pattern names and numbers, meticulously recording the different coloring of each pattern.

"Larkspur" proved popular with the public and was produced in a wide selection of colors and, later, adapted for use as a textile. Customers wishing to experiment with different patterns were able to take home swatches of fabric and a "table book" from the firm's Oxford Street showroom, containing over a hundred examples of Morris & Co. hand-printed papers, each marked on the back with the pattern name and price. All papers, they were assured were "free from arsenic."

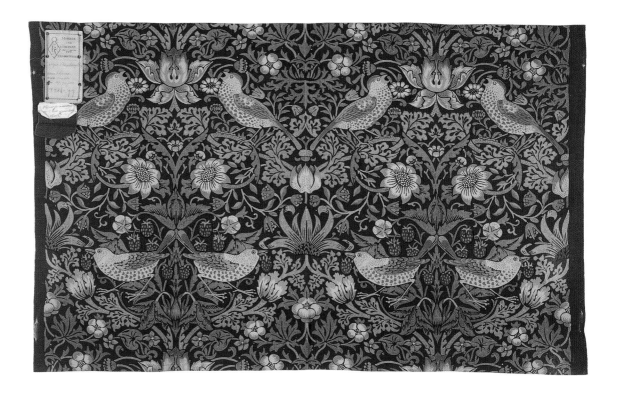

LEFT: The original pencil and watercolor design by William Morris for his "Vine" wallpaper, first issued in 1874, is inscribed with his instructions.

RIGHT: William Morris enlisted the help of Philip Webb, who drew the birds in this design for a furnishing fabric entitled "Strawberry Thief." First registered on May 11, 1883, it went on to become one of Morris's most successful creations.

"You must decide for yourself whether the room most wants stability and repose, or if it is too stiff and formal. If repose be wanted, choose the pattern, other things being considered, which has a horizontal arrangement of its parts. If too great a rigidity be the fault, choose a pattern with soft easy line, either boldly circular or oblique wavy – say 'Scroll', 'Vine', 'Pimpernel', 'Fruit'."

Some of Morris's wallpaper designs, such as the lovely "Larkspur," proved versatile enough to be adapted as textiles, but Morris was so full of ideas that he hardly had need to repeat himself, and almost all his designs were conceived with a particular application in mind. He found inspiration for his textile designs in his usual place: the natural world. "I . . . must have unmistakable suggestions of gardens and fields and strange trees, boughs and tendrils," he wrote. "Strawberry Thief" was based on his direct observation of the behavior of the greedy thrushes in his own garden at Kelmscott Manor. May Morris invites us to imagine the scene: "You can picture my father going out in the early morning and watching the rascally thrushes at work on the fruitbeds, and telling the gardener, who growls 'I'd like to wring their necks!', that no bird in the garden must be touched."

Morris used pattern to create depth and interest in an interior, and understood instinctively how each would work flat on a wall or falling in pleats from a curtain rail, insisting that "No pattern should be without some sort of meaning," though he also championed "a certain mystery." "We should not be able to read the whole thing at once, nor desire to do so, nor be impelled by that desire to go on tracing line after line to find out how the pattern is made," he wrote. A paper such as "Vine," for example, obeys his rule, which states that "the more mysteriously you interweave your sprays and stems the better for your purpose, as the whole thing has to be pasted flat on a wall."

Of all her father's fabric designs, "Honeysuckle" was May Morris's favorite. She described it as "the most truly Morrisian in character of all his pattern-making . . . the most mysterious and poetic – the very symbol of a garden tangle." He preferred a design made the following year based upon the delicate fritillaria, a wildflower native to the watermeadows round Kelmscott Manor. "The single piece of "Snakes-head" that came up last week was very good," he wrote approvingly to Thomas Wardle, "I don't know that I don't like it best of all that we have done."

In Morris's lifetime, his firm Morris & Co. grew into a flourishing and fashionable decorating business, renowned for its wallpapers and textiles. Today, Morris's strong, rhythmic, and balanced patterns, and his ideas about taste and style, are more widely appreciated than ever. In the history of the decorative arts, no other designer has achieved such lasting impact.

CHAPTER FOUR

COMFORT AND CRAFT

ARTS & CRAFTS FURNITURE

LEFT: The Tapestry
Room at Kelmscott
Manor. In the
foreground, a prime
example of one of the
most popular Morris &
Co. products—the
black adjustable
armchair—and behind
that, Morris's writing
desk, inlaid with bone,
originally from his
study at Hammersmith.

ABOVE RIGHT: *William
Morris* by Cosmo
Rowe. This portrait
was painted a year
before Morris died.

As for movable furniture . . . don't have too much of it; have none

for mere finery's sake, or to satisfy the claims of custom — these

are flat truisms, are they not? But really it seems as if some people

had never thought of them for 'tis almost the universal custom to

stuff up some rooms so that you can scarcely move in them."

WILLIAM MORRIS, "MAKING THE BEST OF IT," 1880

WALTER CRANE admired Morris for the revolution he had spearheaded in interior design, ousting "the castored and padded couch from the fireside" and driving the custom of "graining and marbling [interior woodwork] to the public-house." He applauded the way blue and white Nankin, Delft, or Grès de Flandres china had "routed Dresden and Sèvres from the cabinet," and welcomed the plain oak boards and trestles that had replaced "the heavy mahogany telescopic British dining-table of the mid-nineteenth century." Morris himself famously divided furniture into two types—"the necessary work-a-day furniture . . . simple to the last degree" and elaborate, ornamented "state furniture . . . sideboards, cabinets and the like"—and then brought the two types together under the heading of "good citizen's furniture."

A round table, some "colossal" chairs, and a vast settle, which proved too large to transport up the stairs to the unfurnished first-floor student rooms he shared at 17 Red Lion Square with Edward Burne-Jones and had to be winched in through a window, were among the first things Morris ever designed. He was moved to do so by his disenchantment with the shoddiness of the mass-produced furniture he found on offer, and his utter rejection of the prevailing Empire and Rococo styles of heavily embellished domestic furniture. Burne-Jones was impressed: "Topsy has had some furniture (chairs and table) made after his own design; they are as beautiful as mediaeval work, and when we have painted

designs of knights and ladies upon them they will be perfect marvels." They were certainly sturdy pieces, simple constructive forms, handmade from Morris's designs by a local cabinetmaker, and exemplified his preference for furniture "made of timber rather than walking-sticks."

When Morris married Jane Burden in Oxford in the spring of 1859, his collection of hand-painted furniture was swelled by the addition of Philip Webb and Edward Burne-Jones's joint wedding present, a massive wardrobe, designed by Webb, and painted by Burne-Jones with a scene from Chaucer's *Prioress's Tale*. The wardrobe moved with the Morrises from house to house, creating a starting point for the furnishing of Red House, and giving a focus and direction to the distinctive style of furniture produced by Morris, Marshall, Faulkner & Co. from its inception in 1861. Morris wanted honest furniture, "solid and well made in workmanship, [which] in design should have nothing about it that is not easily defensible, no monstrosities or extravagances, not even of beauty, lest we weary of it."

Ford Madox Brown, Rossetti, and Webb were the firm's principle furniture designers in the early days. Madox Brown already had some experience of designing simple and robust furniture for Charles Seddon and Company, and is credited with originating the green stain for oak furniture that was so generally used for Art Furniture. As "one of the earliest and most convinced pioneers in the way of furniture and furnishings both artistic and practical," he made an important contribution to the early progress of the firm, designing unpretentious plain pieces, concentrating on "adaption to need, solidity, a kind of homely beauty and above all absolute dissociation from all false display, veneering and the like." Rossetti found romance in English country designs of the mid-eighteenth century, while Webb's pieces were more elaborate and more Gothic in style, taking their lead from the pioneering work of Augustus Pugin, William Burges, and G. E. Street. Both Webb and Morris knew Street's work well, of course, because they had trained together in his architectural practice in Oxford.

The famous "Morris" chair, which has become such an icon of the Arts & Crafts Movement, was first marketed in 1866 by Morris, Marshall, Faulkner & Co. The prototype was discovered by Warington Taylor, the firm's manager, in the Herstmonceux workshop of an old carpenter named Ephraim Colman, and adapted from the rough sketch Taylor made by Philip Webb, who designed the armchair to incorporate a movable back that could be set at different angles. Morris sold the easy chair in two versions, plain or ebonized wood with a button-backed cushioned seat, covered either in chintz or "Utrecht velvet"—an embossed mohair plush recommended by Christopher Dresser in his *Principles of Decorative Design* (1873) and sold by the firm for use as a wall covering or upholstery material in several colorways. The "Morris" chair proved immensely popular and was widely copied by Liberty, Heal's, and Gustav Stickley's workshops in the United States, where Morris's influence was profound. American agents were successfully selling Morris & Co. products by the late 1870s, and by 1901 Gustav

Stickley was offering seven "Morris" chair models, with minor differences in design, through *The Craftsman*.

Taylor, who shared Morris's social conscience, had also been the impetus behind the firm's hugely popular range of vernacular, rush-seated "Sussex" chairs. "It is hellish wickedness," he wrote, "to spend more than 15 shillings on a chair when the poor are starving in the streets." Taylor wanted the firm to offer "movable furniture . . . something you can pull about with one hand," and accordingly marketed the "Sussex" chairs at reasonable prices in a number of styles: as a corner chair, an armchair, a settle, and a chair with a round seat. "Sussex" chairs were produced in plain or ebonized wood with natural rush seating, and one with a lyre-back was based on a provincial French model and known as the "Rossetti" chair.

Morris used the "Sussex" chairs at Red House, and Burne-Jones ordered a set of black chairs with rush seats for his first married quarters in Great Russell Street, along with one of the firm's solid oak tables, made by apprentices from the Euston Road Boys' Home.

THE SUSSEX CHAIR (1865)

LEFT AND RIGHT:
Two armchairs from
the Sussex range.

"OF ALL THE SPECIFIC MINOR improvements in common household objects due to Morris, the rush-bottomed Sussex chair perhaps takes the first place," wrote J. W. Mackail in his *Life of William Morris*, explaining: "It was not his own invention, but was copied with trifling improvements from an old chair of village manufacture picked up in Sussex. With or without modification it has been taken up by all the modern furniture manufacturers, and is in almost universal use. But the Morris pattern of the later type (there were two) still excels all others in simplicity and elegance of proportion."

The sturdy Sussex chair—first marketed in 1865—soon became a staple of the firm, a cult object for the middle classes and a symbol of Morris himself. Together with the "Daisy" wallpaper it remained in production throughout the firm's existence and retailed for just seven shillings (35 pence) at the turn of the century.

Ford Madox Brown had been the original enthusiast for quasi-peasant furniture (though Rossetti, too, yearned towards a certain "sweet simplicity"), explaining in a letter of 1861 to William Allingham that, at the firm, they did not intend to compete with the expensive products of Messrs. Crace but instead "give real good taste at the price as far as possible of ordinary furniture."

For the firm's newly appointed manager, Warington Taylor, the plain Sussex chair was "essentially gentlemanly" and possessed "poetry of simplicity." The firm marketed a Sussex range, including a triple-seater settle (which retailed at 35 shillings—equivalent to £1.75—and was recommended by Robert Edis in his *Decoration and Furniture of Town Houses* for use in halls), armchairs, a corner seat, and a slightly more elaborate version of the plain chair. There was also a Sussex chair with a round seat, credited to Ford Madox Brown.

Taylor was able to keep prices low because the firm produced and sold very large quantities of the chairs, which were popular not just in private homes, but also institutions. They were used, for example, at Cambridge in the hall of Newnham College, and the Fitzwilliam Museum. Both Liberty and Heal copied the design.

ABOVE: The low-ceilinged hall at Kelmscott Manor retains the original fireplace, flanked by faded hangings of Morris's "Strawberry Thief" chintz. A collection of Iznik plates and tiles is housed in the corner cupboard.

RIGHT: Rossetti's soft pastel drawings of the Morris girls, made in 1871 when Jenny was ten and May nine, hang above two Sussex chairs on either side of an ebonized "whatnot," designed by Webb and made by Morris, Marshall, Faulkner & Co. (*c.* 1860).

The "Sussex" range proved popular with the public and was recommended in contemporary books such as *Decoration and Furniture of Town Houses* (1881) as "excellent comfortable and artistic . . . although somewhat rough in make." A set of "Sussex" chairs was generally to be found in design-conscious homes and in the studios of artists such as Burne-Jones and Alfred Gilbert—as well as in the dining room of Castle Howard in Yorkshire.

Morris made furniture to be used, and he shunned the clutter of the Victorian period. He was not interested in occasional tables designed to display useless objects, and consequently there was less furniture in the interiors he decorated than in typical Victorian rooms, creating more space. The furniture was neither somber nor heavy. To a Victorian eye the result probably looked casual, informal, and decidedly avant-garde. Morris's ideas were rigorous but admitted—indeed, insisted upon—the possibility of beauty. He understood the connection between beauty and usefulness, form and function, and sought to capture the generous and inclusive spirit of medieval times in his furniture, without slavishly copying it. He had a hearty dislike of reproduction furniture, indeed of "fakery" of any kind.

The signature "Morris" chair was still being made by the firm in 1913 and advertised through their catalog at the reasonable price of 10 guineas, or £8 with the less-expensive cotton covers. Other bestsellers included writing tables and a Webb-designed sideboard of painted and ebonized wood with leather panels. Several versions

LEFT: Philip Webb designed this sideboard for Morris, Marshall, Faulkner & Co. in 1862. It is made from ebonized wood, with painted decoration and panels of stamped leather.

RIGHT: Morris's enormous white settle was originally designed for his rooms in Red Lion Square, but Philip Webb adapted it and made it the centerpiece of the first-floor drawing room at Red House. He added a canopy, creating a miniature "minstrel's gallery," which also, rather more prosaically, provided access to the doors leading into the roof-space behind.

of the canopy-topped settle Webb designed for Red House were made by the firm, some with gilt gesso decoration by Charles Faulkner's sister Kate, and others with painted decoration by J. H. Dearle. These were relatively expensively priced at £35 with embossed leather panels, or £30 undecorated, in the firm's catalog. Most of Webb's early furniture for the firm was made of plain oak, often stained black or green, or decorated with gesso, oil paint, or lacquer.

Much of the early furniture was made in Great Ormond Yard, just around the corner from Queen Square, although, after 1881, furniture manufacture—along with tapestry and wallpaper production—moved to the larger workshops at Merton Abbey in Surrey. Nine years later a new furniture factory in Pimlico was acquired from Holland & Son, and this flourished under the management of George Jack, formerly assistant to Philip Webb and well known for his work as a carver. Jack became Chief Designer for Morris & Co. in 1890 and, together with W. A. S. Benson, took over the commercial side of the firm's furniture production after

Morris's death, in 1896. He was responsible for many of the elaborate and highly finished monumental mahogany or walnut "state" pieces, often with inlaid decoration, which became associated with the firm, such as the dining room table with herringbone inlay for Alexander Ionides' Holland Park home and the glass-fronted cabinet in the drawing room. Later versions of this were described in the Morris & Co. catalog as "of highest Sheraton finish," a description Morris would have found distasteful and one that demonstrates how far the firm had moved from the vernacular style exemplified by Webb's plain, heavy, functional "joiner-made" pieces to ride the popular wave of Georgian revival designs.

It could be argued that, after 1896, furniture production by the firm moved away from Morris's highest ideals, and that these were then upheld by a number of important Arts & Crafts practitioners who were old friends, associates or protégés of Morris. Among them were men such as Arthur Heygate Mackmurdo, W. R. Lethaby, and Ernest Gimson. Mackmurdo

LEFT: This Gimson rocking chair incorporates the distinctive ladderback design.

LEFT: This Gimson rocking chair incorporates the distinctive ladderback design.

RIGHT: The dining room of the Irving House in Illinois, designed by Frank Lloyd Wright in 1909.

viewed the Arts & Crafts Movement "not as an aesthetic excursion; but as a mighty upheaval of man's spiritual nature" and shared Morris's belief in the dignity and joy of labor, with an emphasis on handcrafted methods and honesty to function and material. In 1882 he formed the Century Guild, with the aim of supplying all the furniture and other furnishings necessary for a house and, most importantly, involving the artist in the areas of work previously considered the realm of tradesmen. Mackmurdo wanted to restore craftsmanship to its rightful place "beside painting and sculpture." Like Morris, he had mastered several crafts, including brasswork, embroidery, and cabinetmaking and, along with distinctive furniture—chairs, desks, sofas, and cabinets—he designed buildings, metalwork, wallpapers, and textiles.

Similarly, in an attempt to break down barriers between artists and architects, and designers and craftsmen, W. R. Lethaby founded the Art Workers' Guild in 1884. This led to the formation of the Arts & Crafts Exhibition Society, with Walter Crane as its first chairman, and a committee that included William Morris and Edward Burne-Jones. The Society organized regular lectures, practical demonstrations, and annual exhibitions in the New Gallery on Regent Street, providing a useful shop window for Arts and Craft Movement designers such as Sidney Barnsley, Ernest Gimson, Reginald Blomfield, Ford Madox Brown, George Jack, and C. R. Ashbee, who later opened his own shop on Brook Street, displaying the work of his Guild of Handicraft. All exhibitors had to satisfy strict criteria, the most important of which was that their work was entirely handmade. The furniture on show was unlike anything commercially produced at the time and, as *The Builder* noted, seemed to "have been done because the designer and maker enjoyed doing them, not because they were calculated to sell well."

Lethaby, Gimson, Sidney Barnsley, and his brother Ernest also went on to set up the short-lived but highly influential firm of Kenton & Co., very much in the spirit of Morris's venture, which produced some striking pieces of handcrafted furniture, a characteristically

geometric style, and a method of surface decoration very similar to Shaker designs. In keeping with the Arts & Crafts belief that a workman inevitably produced better work and gained more personal satisfaction from seeing a single job through from start to finish, each piece was made by a single craftsman and his contribution was acknowledged, along with the designer's, with initials impressed into the wood with a simple metal stamp.

When the firm folded, Gimson and the Barnsleys moved to the Cotswolds, where they made ladderback chairs and solidly constructed furniture with open joinery, in the direct tradition of William Morris, Philip Webb, and Ford Madox Brown. They worked with local woods—oak, elm, ash, deal, and fruitwoods—which they left unadorned or chose to decorate simply by chamfering the wood, and attracted praise and censure in equal measures: "The object now seems to be to make a thing as square, as plain, as devoid of any beauty of line as is possible and to call this art," complained *The Builder* in 1899. However, this simple type of furniture was

attractive to many and led to the new integrated interior, since pieces such as dressers, window seats, and settles were built in.

Innovative architects such as M. H. Baillie Scott, Charles Voysey, Charles Rennie Mackintosh, and Frank Lloyd Wright were designing furniture from the same materials and finishes as the houses themselves, relating everything to the whole so that "all are speaking the same language." They created dramatic open-plan interiors that revolutionized the use of space, leading to a greater sense of informality and flexibility. The Arts & Crafts house, with its emphasis on space, light, air, and honest decoration had truly arrived. The architects used local materials and local craftsmen, and concerned themselves with every aspect of the design of a house, with the result that the interiors they created were coherent and deeply satisfying. Their love of wood was immediately apparent in the paneling, high-backed oak settles built into inglenooks, and distinctive freestanding pieces of furniture, which were often covered in Morris fabric. There was evidence of

LEFT: An elegant oak sideboard from Heal & Son's.

RIGHT: A period room in Liberty's department store, with original wood-paneling, furniture, and metalwork from Liberty's early twentieth-century Arts & Crafts ranges.

painstaking craftsmanship throughout each house, in the exposed details on wooden staircases, ceiling beams, carved panels, and studded and strap-hinged plain plank doors.

Large companies such as Heal's and Liberty that had been quick to imitate the innovative style of Morris, now adopted the Arts & Crafts look wholesale, often undercutting prices, and eventually bringing about the demise of C. R. Ashbee's Chipping Campden Guild of Handicraft. Arthur Lazenby Liberty was a shrewd businessman, with his finger on the fashionable pulse, who set out to provide furniture and furnishings that would meet the demand for "aesthetic" interiors. He promoted a style that combined commercial Art Nouveau with the design vocabulary of the Arts & Crafts Movement. Liberty both "borrowed" from Arts & Crafts designers (his own range was clearly influenced by Morris and Voysey) and commissioned them as well. He shamelessly exploited the visual appeal and emotional resonance of the Arts & Crafts ideal of traditional workmanship, without the high cost of individual

craft production, and traded on the Arts & Crafts ethic while ignoring its social message. It is perhaps ironic that Liberty was responsible for introducing a wider public to a diluted version of the ideals of Morris and the Arts & Crafts Movement, while simultaneously hastening the Movement's end.

Ambrose Heal, who was a designer himself, was more in tune with the ideals of the Arts & Crafts Movement, though he was unembarrassed about using modern methods. "The machine," he wrote, "relieves the workman of a good deal of drudgery and legitimately cheapens production." This was an important point, since the Arts & Crafts Movement's insistence on handcrafted artifacts meant that most of the pieces it produced were beyond the means of the very people intended to benefit from their "improving" presence in their homes. Heal & Son's "Plain Oak Furniture" and "Simple Bedroom Furniture" ranges enabled earnest young couples to fill their homes with the kind of pieces their reading of William Morris's *News From Nowhere* had made them

yearn for. The furniture was bought enthusiastically by a wide range of customers—including Margaret Beale who installed Heal's beds at Standen.

As well as the rich cross-fertilization of British and continental European design ideas, the Arts & Crafts style and ideals were enthusiastically adopted in the United States, where Gustav Stickley was one of their main promoters. Profoundly influenced by Morris, Ruskin, Voysey, and Ashbee, he had returned from an epiphanic trip to England in 1898, determined to spread the message, writing:

> "I felt that the badly constructed, over-ornate, meaningless furniture that was turned out in such quantities by the factories was not only bad in itself, but that its presence in the homes of the people was an influence that led directly away from the sound qualities which make an honest man and a good citizen."

Stickley established his own guild of artisans, United Crafts, in Eastwood, New York, and developed his own "Mission" style of home furnishings, which Americans could order through his mail-order catalogs. The range included textiles, lamps, and carpets, and chairs based on Morris's signature design, which he patented in 1901. He described the largest model as "a big, deep chair that means comfort to a tired man when he comes home after the day's work."

Stickley published a magazine called *The Craftsman* to publicize his philosophy and products, and in the first two issues ran long appreciations of William Morris and John Ruskin. He wanted to produce "a simple, democratic art" that would provide Americans with "material surroundings conducive to plain living and high thinking." He intended "to do away with all needless ornamentation, returning to plain principles of construction and applying them to the making of simple, strong, comfortable furniture."

Stickley was unrepentant about his businesslike approach, and used the latest machinery to make "oak furniture that shows plainly

ABOVE: An oak "drop-arm" spindle Morris chair, marketed by Gustav Stickley in the early part of the twentieth century.

LEFT: An illustration from *The Craftsman*, showing the dining room with a built-in sideboard and recessed window in one of Gustav Stickley's ideal Craftsman houses.

what it is, and in which the design and construction harmonize with the wood." He based his simple squat forms on seventeenth-century colonial furniture, intending to evoke the "simple life" of the early American settlers, and these proved very successful. He employed talented designers such as Harvey Ellis, who took the furniture side of the firm in a direction inspired by Charles Rennie Mackintosh, making lighter, more elegant, but unfortunately more easily copied furniture.

Another important outlet for American Arts & Crafts furniture during the same period was provided by the craftsmen at Elbert Hubbard's Roycroft Arts & Crafts community in East Aurora, New York, founded in 1892 with the ideal of a return to the simple life of preindustrial America. The Roycrofters built their own shops, studios, and houses according to principles of communal living. The furniture they produced was heavy and solid, not unlike Stickley's "Mission" style pieces, though more Gothic in manner. This characteristic was underscored by the Gothic-style carved letters of the Roycroft name, and by the orb and double-barred cross symbol with which the ash, mahogany or dark, fumed oak pieces were marked.

CHAPTER FIVE

THE SOFTER ELEMENTS

CURTAINS, CARPETS, RUGS, SCREENS, AND WALL HANGINGS

LEFT: The Indian Bird bedroom at Wightwick Manor, showing the Morris & Co. velvet hangings on the bedstead, which is made up from pieces of Jacobean carving.

ABOVE RIGHT: William Morris in his study at Kelmscott House. May recalled how her father used to work against the background noise of local children playing on the scrubbed steps of his front door until he could endure it no longer and then he would "go out and beg them to give him a little peace and quiet and play elsewhere for a while."

"I think it is desirable that the artist and what is technically called the designer should practically be one. . . A designer ought to be able to weave himself."

WILLIAM MORRIS, EVIDENCE TO THE ROYAL COMMISSION ON TECHNICAL INSTRUCTION, 1882

WILLIAM MORRIS NEVER DESIGNED a textile without giving careful thought to how it was to be used and the best technique to suit this purpose. He understood his material, knew how each fabric would fall or drape or stretch across the seat of a chair, and he knew how to achieve the right depth of color. In an article entitled "Textiles," published in 1893, he urged his readers to:

> "Never forget the material you are working with, and try always to use it for what it can do best: if you feel yourself hampered with the material in which you are working, instead of being helped by it, you have so far not learned your business."

Morris himself learned through doing, working doggedly at each new technique until he had mastered and understood it entirely. Morris's degree of involvement was total, as May Morris explains:

LEFT: Morris's woven woollen "Peacock and Dragon" fabric design (1878).

RIGHT: The "Daisy" wall hanging, designed by Morris in 1860 and worked by his wife Jane on a length of indigo serge.

"He was in direct relation with the silk-weavers and carpet-weavers, dyers and blockers, with pattern-makers and block-cutters, with cabinet makers and carvers in wood; with glass painters, kiln men and labourers and with his wall-paper printers; and it was not as if he sat in an office and received reports from managers of different departments with the technical details of which he was unfamiliar: he had grasped the nature of those he employed – understanding their limitations as well as their capabilities."

Morris came to textile design through an early interest in embroidery, dating back to his bohemian Red Lion Square years, when, just out of Oxford, he was sharing "the quaintest rooms in all London, hung with brasses of old knights and drawings of Albert [sic] Durer" with Edward Burne-Jones and experimenting with various artistic techniques. It was a curiously male world of camaraderie and practical jokes, late hours, and unrestrained freedom and friendliness. Visitors described the "noble confusion" of Morris's room, chaotically packed with monumental pieces of furniture, broken fragments of Flemish or Italian pottery, stray suits of armor, half-finished pictures, and sketchbooks. In a corner was a wooden embroidery frame that Morris had copied from an old example, and on which, with his usual painstaking patience and determination, he taught himself the art of embroidery by unpicking old examples to discover how they had been made. It was all part of his desire to recreate an English medieval interior.

Morris soon enlisted the aid of his housekeeper, Mary Nicholson, known as Red Lion Mary, teaching her the stitches he had only just mastered himself. A year later he sketched out a simple daisy design for his wife, Jane, to work on a piece of indigo-dyed blue serge she had found by chance in a London shop. "He was delighted with it," Jane wrote, "and set to work at once designing flowers – these we

worked in bright colours in a simple, rough way – the work went quickly and when we finished we covered the walls of the bedroom at Red House to our great joy."

Jane's work won a medal at the 1862 exhibition, but the *Clerical Journal* was scornful:

> "Middle class people do not use hangings of any kind upon their walls and are not likely to furnish their drawing rooms, or even their bedrooms, with such homely-looking material as this … we should be a little surprised to see the material in actual use anywhere except in the quaintly-furnished bachelor rooms of an artist, or the private snuggery of a mediaevalist."

Undeterred, Morris, who had by now taught Jane's sister Bessie Burden to embroider as well, concentrated on producing designs for an ambitious scheme for a dozen woolen hangings he had devised

for the drawing room of Red House, depicting females figures— "Illustrious Women" drawn from the works of Chaucer—which had the same bold black outlines as stained glass. Later he undertook elaborate commissions for embroidered panels, often based on Chaucerian themes, for wealthy customers such as Sir Isaac Lowthian Bell, whose house—Rounton Grange, Northallerton, in Yorkshire—was designed and built by Philip Webb.

Morris's "Romaunt de la Rose" series was embroidered in silks, wools, and gold thread by Lady Bell and her daughters Florence and Ada Phoebe, just as Margaret Beale and her daughters worked Morris's complicated "Artichoke" over a period of years for their Sussex weekend house, Standen—another Philip Webb commission—for which Morris & Co. supplied many of the interior furnishings. Soon Morris & Co. were offering embroidery kits with the pattern ready-traced on silk for customers to make into their own cushion covers, workbags, or fire screens. These items could also be bought ready-made from the shop.

LEFT: An unfinished embroidery kit, partially worked silks on a cotton ground, bought from Morris & Co. (*c.* 1890).

FAR RIGHT: This elaborate table cover, embroidered in silks on linen by May Morris *c.* 1885, was bought by Laurence Hodson, a Midlands brewer, for Compton Hall, his house near Wolverhampton, which Morris & Co. decorated.

In 1885 Morris put his younger daughter May in charge of the embroidery section of the firm. After May's marriage to Henry Halliday Sparling, the Secretary of the Socialist League, her team of embroideresses—which included Lily Yeats, sister of the poet; Mary de Morgan, sister of the potter; and Mrs. George Jack, wife of the firm's chief furniture designer—worked at her house at 8 Hammersmith Terrace, just a short walk from her father's Kelmscott House. May was just twenty-three when she took on the management of the department that grew under her direction to become a significant arm of the firm, producing wall hangings, bedspreads, curtains, tablecloths, fire screens, portieres (door curtains, used to exclude drafts and insulate a room), and bed and cushion covers. The embroidery was sold as kits, partially started or as finished pieces. May traveled to the United States for a lecture tour, from the winter of 1909 to the spring of 1910, and her work found its way across the Atlantic, when a set of bed-hangings with designs of birds and foliage, displayed at the Detroit Society of Arts & Crafts Exhibition, in 1920, was bought by George Booth, a newspaper magnate from Detroit, for his house in Michigan.

In 1875 Morris took the opportunity offered by Thomas Wardle—the brother-in-law of the firm's manager George Wardle—to experiment with vegetables at his dye-house in Leek, in Staffordshire. The two men collaborated on patterns and color schemes, consulting old herbals, scouring Pliny's *Historia Naturalis* for ideas, and reviving Elizabethan recipes for dyes. Morris pondered the problem constantly: "I was at Kelmscott the other day," he wrote to Wardle in November, "in that beautiful cold weather and betwixt fishing, I cut a handful of poplar twigs and boiled them, and dyed a lock of wool a very good yellow: this would be useful if fast, for the wool was unmordanted."

Color had always been central to Morris's vision, and for some time now he had been "deeply impressed with the importance of our having all our dyes the soundest and best that can be." Disenchanted with chemical dyes, which produced "hideous colours, crude, livid and cheap" and, worse, faded unevenly and were apt to discolor, he returned to the old animal and vegetable dyes in his attempt to achieve the rich colors of the old tapestries and fabrics he so loved. It was a long, laborious process of trial and error, and Morris loved it. In a letter to Aglaia Coronio, he states:

> "I am working in Mr. Wardle's dye-house in sabots and blouse pretty much all day long. I am dyeing yellows and reds: the yellows are very easy to get, and so are a lot of shades of salmon and flesh colour and buff and orange; my chief difficulty is in getting a deep blood red, but I hope to succeed before I come away."

Morris did, indeed, succeed. W. R. Lethaby described a Morris fabric as appearing as if it was "stained through and through with the juices of flowers." The recipes in the Merton Abbey dye book, often accompanied by a fabric sample, demonstrate the huge amount of effort and time that went into achieving exactly the right result.

The restructuring of the firm had proved an expensive, acrimonious, and bruising business for Morris who, in March 1875, told Charles Fairfax Murray (then working as an assistant in Edward Burne-Jones's studio) that he was "scraping everything together to pay my thieves of partners." The solution to his troubles, as ever for Morris, lay in work, and plenty of it. He resolved to make Morris & Co. even better by giving his customers more choice. "I am up to the neck in turning out designs for paper, chintzes and carpets and trying to get the manufacturers to do them," he wrote to Fairfax Murray in May. During the decade that followed he created twenty-one new designs for wallpapers, twenty-three for woven fabrics, thirty-two for printed fabrics, and dozens for machine and handmade carpets, tapestries, and embroideries, causing W. R. Lethaby to hail him as "the greatest pattern-designer we ever had or ever can have."

Color was usually the starting point for Morris's interior design schemes with the predominant color for the room represented on the walls and woodwork, and the "subordinate or auxiliary color" in the soft furnishings. He recommended using curtain material that would "blend, or harmonise with the walls and help to surround the

RIGHT: Morris worked on this design at Kelmscott House while suffering from gout. In a letter to May, dated Saturday March 3, 1883, he explained how he came to name it: "I have been at work pretty hard & have made a new pattern which in honour of the occasion I ought to call 'Colchium': only as Colchium is nothing less than a crocus & I have stupidly omitted to put a crocus in, to avoid questions being asked I must fall back on a river and call it Evenlode."

OPPOSITE: The painted ceiling of the studio on the first floor of Red House, with its high rafters and windows overlooking the garden.

carpet with a frame of colour," and understood how the rhythm and movement of the chosen pattern would resonate within the room. In a brochure published by the firm in 1888, Morris wrote:

> "Chairs and sofas give great opportunities for introducing points of bright contrasting colour, and for those high lights and darkest shades which are essential in a complete scheme. Covers need not be uniform. They may be of two or three or four kinds, according to the size of the room and the number of pieces."

The cleaner lines of our contemporary interiors would have met with Morris's approval. His stated aim was to do away with unnecessary clutter, and he wished to sweep away the "tons upon tons of unutterable rubbish pretending to be works of art in some degree" in London houses, leaving only what was useful and

beautiful. However, he understood the impact that could be made by the strategic use of pattern and color.

Morris often used windows for dramatic effect, hanging curtains in "shades of red that would brighten all up without fighting with the wall hangings" in Rosalind Howard's boudoir in her London house, but choosing simple white, wool curtains for the drawing room of his own country house, Kelmscott Manor. In general, he popularized simpler curtain treatments. In place of the complicated and fussy multiple layers, festooned, braided, and topped by an elaborate pelmet or "ormolu battering-ram," came loosely pleated curtains, often hung in full folds from a slender black wood or light brass curtain rod, or even a "steel bronzed" brass pole—a much lighter style with which we are at home today. Curtains, lined with a toning cotton or contrasting pattern to present a lively face to the outside world, were made up for Morris & Co. customers in "a large rambling old building, wooden from top to bottom and gas lit," just around the corner from the Oxford

LEFT: William Morris gave this hand-knotted rug to Margaret Burne-Jones, daughter of the artist, as a present on the occasion of her wedding to John William Mackail in 1888. His letter, dated August 21, explains: "I have bidden our Mr Smith to send you an 'article' called a Hammersmith rug which Janey and I ask you to take as a small and unimportant addition to your 'hards.'"

RIGHT: A pencil and watercolor design by William Morris for "Quatre foil" carpet.

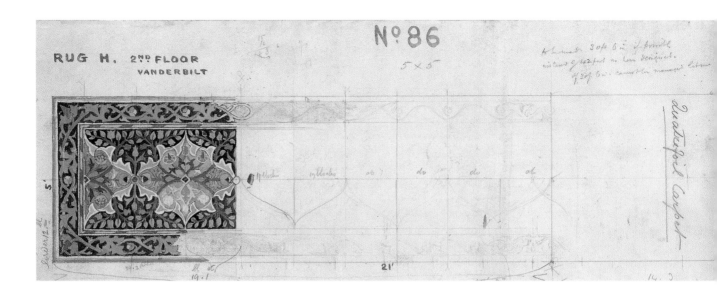

Street showroom, where matching braid and tasseled tiebacks and tasseled cords were on sale.

In "The Lesser Arts of Life" (1882), Morris urged people to choose a beautiful pattern "that will not drive us either to unrest or into callousness" but "reminds us of life beyond itself, and which has the impress of human imagination strong upon it." Passionate about pattern, he wanted his own to be beautiful and meaningful, soothing and suggestive, fresh and original. In the 1880s he named a series of patterns for textile designs after tributaries of the Thames—"Cray," "Medway," "Kennet," and "Evenlode"—reflecting his lifelong love of rivers and streams.

Morris's great gift was for color and pattern, but he also knew how to use texture to achieve effect and designed patterns for woven materials, using mixtures of cotton, linen, wool, velveteen, silk, and mohair, to create depth and lend versatility. Before the advent of Morris's approach, the convention had been to change loose covers and curtains with the season, using plush and heavy velvets in the winter and lighter washable cotton covers in the summer. Morris's printed chintzes popularized cotton as a year-round, rather than merely summer, upholstery fabric.

Fabulous carpets designed by Morris and produced in Hammersmith were individual works of art and often the crowning glory of his largest decorative schemes, such as at 1 Holland Park, Clouds, Naworth, Rounton Grange, and Bullerswood. However, when

Morris made his first experiments in hand-knotting carpets, carefully studying an antique Persian carpet until he understood how it had been made, hand-knotted carpets were not being manufactured in Britain at all. His first attempts were made on a frame set up in an attic at Queen Square but, following the move to Kelmscott House, he installed several carpet frames in a large coach house and stable, hence the firm's handmade carpets gained their "Hammersmith" label.

The widest carpet frame was for a twelve-foot carpet, and each of the six young women Morris employed was expected to knot two inches of carpet each day. It was a slow, expensive process and put Morris's individually commissioned handmade carpets, like his tapestries, beyond the purse of all but the most wealthy. The middle classes could, however, still cover their floors with Morris & Co. power-loom-woven carpets, which greatly outsold the handmade versions. Morris's machine-made Brussels, Wilton pile, or Kidderminster carpets, competed in a crowded market with large manufacturers such as John Crossley & Son of Halifax, while James Templeton & Co. of Glasgow, the leading firm in Axminsters, gave Morris & Co. a run for their money with their excellent imitation Persian and Turkish carpets.

Wall-to-wall carpeting was rare, and Morris produced square or rectangular carpets with decorative borders intended to be laid over plain, stained, marbled, painted, or occasionally stenciled oak floorboards or parquet flooring. For the central design, "filling," or

ABOVE: William Morris's work found an eager audience in America. This fine example of his "Poppy" carpet graces the drawing room at the Lyman Estate, Society for the Preservation of New England Antiquities, in Waltham, Massachusetts.

"field" Morris aimed "to produce pure and shapely forms with simple colouring . . . without straining its [the carpet's] capacity for decoration," and his Kidderminster carpets in particular proved popular in the United States, where they were sold, through agents, well into the twentieth century. Along with wallpapers and fabrics, carpets were among the most popular items on the Morris & Co. stand at the Foreign Fair held in Boston, and the *The Boston Home Journal* of December 22, 1883 noted approvingly that "the Morris exhibit is rapidly passing into the hands of fortunate Bostonians."

In his own homes, Morris used only oriental carpets and amassed an impressive collection from Turkey, India, and Persia, promising his daughter May in 1876 that his latest purchase of Persian carpets would "make you feel as if you were in the Arabian nights." He hung some of these lovely antique carpets on his walls for inspiration and laid others down on well-swept floors. However, in his 1880 lecture entitled "Making the Best of It," he proposed, daringly, that people should "no longer look upon a carpet as a necessity for a room at all,

at least in the summer," claiming that "it is a great comfort to see the actual floor," and suggesting that the floor might be "made very ornamental by either wood mosaic, or tile and marble mosaic."

For Morris "the noblest of all the weaving arts" was tapestry, and in 1877 he set up a loom in his bedroom at Kelmscott House and rose early each morning to teach himself the techniques that would allow him to realize his "bright dream." He loved tapestry for its "special excellencies . . . crispness and abundance of beautiful detail" and the quality of "a mosaic of pieces of colour made up of dyed threads" that led to a fine "depth of tone, richness of colour and exquisite gradations of tints." Morris, as usual, did the job thoroughly, making a careful study of the historical textiles at the South Kensington Museum (now the Victoria and Albert Museum), where he was particularly taken by the stylized pomegranates and artichokes used as motifs in antique fabrics.

Morris's first tapestry panel took him 516 hours to weave and was known as "Acanthus and Vine," though Morris referred to it

THE FOREST TAPESTRY (1887)

(121.9 × 420.0 CM) DESIGNED BY WILLIAM MORRIS,
PHILIP WEBB AND JOHN HENRY DEARLE

THIS LOVELY LONG RICH TAPESTRY was woven in wool and silk on a cotton warp at the Merton Abbey workshops in 1887 by three of Morris & Co.'s most experienced weavers—William Knight, John Martin, and William Sleath, who with Knight had joined Morris as an apprentice in the 1870s. (John Martin went on to become the first tapestry restorer at the Victoria and Albert Museum.) Morris had a genius for spotting and fostering talent in the young and the weavers were allowed considerable latitude in the interpretation of subtleties of tint and shading, for he maintained that "the executants themselves [are] in both nature and training, artists, not merely animated machines."

Indeed Morris's gifted assistant, John Henry Dearle—who was responsible for the floral details in "The Forest" tapestry—was a case in point. He had been taken on in 1878 because Morris had been "influenced by the evident intelligence and brightness of the boy" and quickly learned and mastered the trade, going on to train the young boys who followed—Morris preferred to employ young boys for tapestry weaving because the work "involves little muscular efforts and is best carried on by small flexible fingers."

"The Forest" is one of Morris's most successful tapestries. A collaborative effort between Morris, Dearle, and Philip Webb, who supplied the five charming pencil drawings of birds and animals, which Morris incorporated into his overall design, arranging the animals peeping through a dense background of trailing acanthus leaves. The poetic inscription emblazoned across the center of the tapestry—"The beasts that be in woodland waste, now sit and see nor ride nor haste"—was later expanded and published under the title "The Lion" in Morris's *Poems by the Way* (1891).

The tapestry was displayed at the 1890 Arts & Crafts Exhibition and bought by Alex Ionides for 1 Holland Park, where it hung in the study, alongside a small subsidiary acanthus-leaf panel. In 1926 the Victoria and Albert Museum purchased the tapestry for £500, £100 of which was donated by the National Art Collections Fund.

as "Cabbage and Vine." He went on to collaborate with Burne-Jones, Philip Webb, and John Henry Dearle on some of the finest tapestries of the period, including "The Forest," which was woven at Merton Abbey, shown at the 1890 Arts & Crafts Exhibition, and purchased by Alexander Ionides to hang in the study of his house at 1 Holland Park. Morris's most famous tapestry, designed entirely by himself and worked by May Morris and her assistants in 1885, was "Woodpecker," inspired by nature and Ovid's *Metamorphoses*. It hung for a number of years in the billiard room of George Prothero, the President of the Royal Historical Society, at 24 Bedford Square, but can now be seen in the William Morris Gallery in Walthamstow.

As the critics had predicted, few could afford to furnish their homes with large tapestries, but small figure panels and cushion covers sold well through Morris & Co.'s showroom and found their way into hundreds of homes. Morris himself had acquired a small collection of his own antique tapestries when he leased Kelmscott Manor in 1871, for one of the rooms was hung with old tapestries narrating the biblical story of Samson and Delilah. Morris acknowledged that "they were never great works of art" but loved to study their faded colors and felt they made "the walls a very pleasant background for the living people who haunt the room" and "give an air of romance which nothing else would quite do."

By the 1880s Morris was well on his way to his goal of offering his customers a large range of products of original design and excellent quality that could be successfully used in combination by anyone interested in interior decoration. From its single retail outlet on Oxford Street and via various overseas agents, Morris & Co. offered scores of designs for wallpapers, textiles, and carpets in colors "carefully chosen to harmonise with our styles of decoration," as well as hand-painted tiles, embroideries, and a large portfolio of designs for furniture.

Prices for wallpaper varied, depending on the number of blocks used in the hand-printing; for printed fabrics, the price was relative to the complexity of the production process. For example, Morris's favorite printed fabric, "Honeysuckle," was one of the firm's most expensive, requiring over a dozen different blocks. Some fabrics, such as the silk velvet "Granada," which featured gilt thread, were simply too expensive, and consequently were deemed commercially unviable. However, other fabrics, such as "Tulip and Rose," and the embossed "Utrecht Velvet," which was a popular covering for the reclining "Morris" chair, were woven on power-looms, rather than the Jacquard loom, and priced to meet the middle-class purse. Customers who could not afford the services of the great man himself nevertheless flocked to Oxford Street to buy wallpapers, fabrics, and carpets, and they constructed their own decorative schemes based on the principles of Morris's designs.

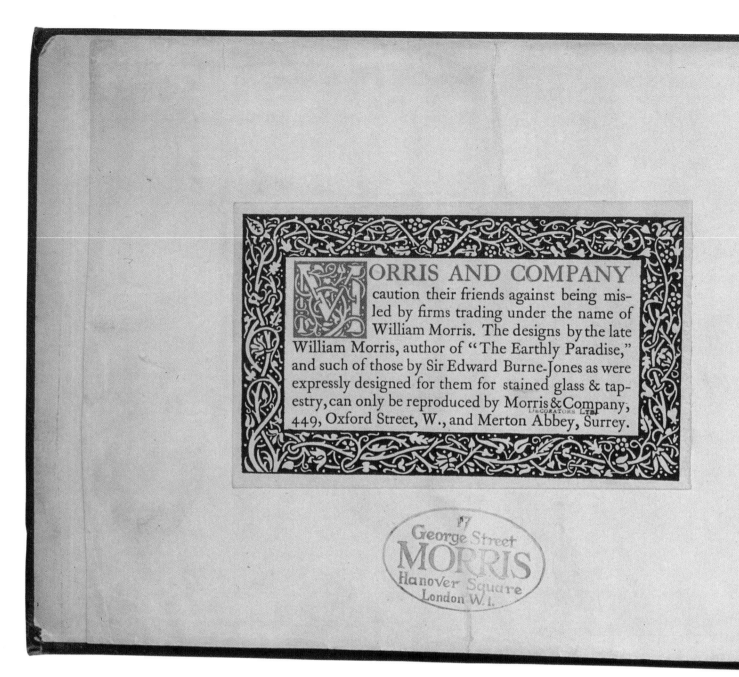

ORRIS AND COMPANY caution their friends against being mis- led by firms trading under the name of William Morris. The designs by the late William Morris, author of "The Earthly Paradise," and such of those by Sir Edward Burne-Jones as were expressly designed for them for stained glass & tap- estry, can only be reproduced by Morris & Company, DECORATORS LTD. 449, Oxford Street, W., and Merton Abbey, Surrey.

FAR LEFT: Morris's "Peacock and Dragon" woven woollen fabric was offered by Morris & Co. from 1878 and proved very popular. Madeleine Wyndham had a set of four curtains made up in it for the hall at Clouds, her country house near Salisbury.

LEFT: Morris's "Violet and Columbine" woven woollen fabric dates from around 1883.

ABOVE: Recognizing the growing popularity of printed velveteens, William Morris wrote to Thomas Wardle in February 1877: "We could have a trade in velvets and serges if we could get the colours good and fast." This sample book of ten printed velveteens—open to show "Acanthus"—offered by Morris & Co. for use as curtaining and upholstery, illustrates just how he met the market.

RIGHT: A photograph of the large drawing room at Kelmscott House, Hammersmith, furnished with the "Prioress's Tale" wardrobe, Philip Webb's early settle, and various other items, including Morris & Co. adjustable chairs.

By 1881 the time had come for the firm to expand, and Morris signed a lease on the Merton Abbey workshops, formerly a silk-weaving factory and print works on the banks of the River Wandle. Morris called it a "place which hangs doubtful between the past and the present"; others referred to it as "a colossal kindergarten for adults." For Morris, it sparked a new burst of creativity. There he was able to set up a dye-house, since the river water was perfect for use in the dyeing process, and pits were dug and lined to make indigo vats. He also set up a weaving factory and glass studio, and installed his carpet looms.

Emma Lazarus, the American poet and essayist, wrote an article entitled "A Day in Surrey with William Morris," which was published in *Century Magazine* in July 1886. After enthusing on the prettiness of the village railway station, she described Morris's operation:

> "In the first outhouse that we entered stood great vats of liquid dye, into which some skeins of unbleached wool were dipped for our amusement; as they were brought dripping forth, they appeared of a sea-green color, but after a few minutes exposure to the air, they settled into a fast, dusky blue. Scrupulous neatness and order reigned everywhere in the establishment; pleasant smells as of dried herbs exhaled from clean vegetable dyes, blent with the wholesome odour of grass and flowers and sunny summer warmth that freely circulated through open doors and windows. Nowhere was one conscious of the depressing sense of confinement that usually pervades a factory; there was plenty of air and light even in the busiest room, filled with the ceaseless din of whirring looms where the artisans sat bending over their threads; while the lovely play of color and beauty of texture of the fabrics issuing from under their fingers relieved their work of that character of purely mechanical drudgery which is one of the dreariest features of ordinary factory toil. Yet this was evidently the department that entailed the most arduous and sedentary labor."

By 1890 the Morris & Co. showrooms offered customers a choice of over fifty wallpaper designs, forty-three printed fabrics and thirty-three designs for woven fabrics. Although Morris had, in 1883, been able to claim, "Almost all the designs we use for surface decoration, wallpapers, textiles and the like, I design myself," now his assistant, John Henry Dearle, was beginning to take on much of this work, since Morris's energies were channeled into his political activities.

WILLIAM MORRIS'S BED AT KELMSCOTT MANOR

W. B. Yeats, she embroidered William's poem, "For the Bed at Kelmscott"—composed the same year—around the vallance, and used his early "Trellis" design as a background pattern for the curtains. Jane embroidered the coverlet, with naturalistic bouquets and a quotation from William's poem "A Garden by the Sea," taken from his epic work *The Life and Death of Jason* (1867). In a nod towards their early years at Red House, she signed it "Si je puis. Jane Morris. Kelmscott." William was so pleased with the final effect that he framed the full-size design for the delicately colored coverlet and hung it beside his bed against the "Daisy" patterned walls.

William loved "the sweet simple old place" enormously and regretted that his busy political schedule prevented him from sleeping in his magnificent bed as often as he might have wished.

Unsurprisingly, given the triangular nature of the early domestic arrangements at Kelmscott Manor, William and Jane Morris maintained separate bedrooms in their country retreat. Both slept in spectacular beds: Jane in an early nineteenth-century mahogany four-poster – in which her husband had been born on 24 March, 1834 at Walthamstow—hung with "Willow" patterned chintz to match the wallpaper; William, across the landing, in a huge, early seventeenth-century, oak four-poster bed, which was about as old as the house itself. The bed dominates the room but what draws the eye, what makes it so striking, is the way it has been decorated. William's daughter May Morris designed and worked the bed hangings in wools on natural-colored linen in 1891. With the help of a number of friends, including Ellen Wright, Maude Deacon, and Lily Yeats, sister of the poet

"The Wind's on the wold and the night is a-cold,
And Thames runs chill twixt mead and hill
But kind and dear is the old house here,
And my heart is warm midst winter's harm.
Rest, then and rest, and think of the best
Twixt summer and spring when all birds sing
In the town of the tree, and ye lie in me
And scare dare move lest earth and its love
Should fade away ere the full of the day.
I am old and have seen many things that have been,
Both grief and peace, and wane and increase.
No tale I tell of ill or well,
But this I say: night treadeth on day,
And for worst and best right good is rest."

CHAPTER SIX

FINISHING TOUCHES

THE SIMPLICITY OF ORNAMENT

"To give people pleasure in the

things they must perforce *use*, that

is one great office of decoration;

to give people pleasure in the things

they must perforce *make*, that is

the other use of it."

WILLIAM MORRIS, "THE LESSER ARTS," 1877

LEFT: Philip Webb designed these two facing fitted dressers for the dining room at Standen himself, but the dining table and chairs were supplied by S. & H. Jewell & Co. in 1894. The seats were embroidered in wool by Margaret Beale and other female members of the family, working from designs supplied by the Royal School of Art Needlework. The curtains were made up in "Peacock and Dragon" woven woollen fabric by the firm in 1897 at a cost of 35 pounds 8 shillings.

ABOVE RIGHT: William Morris's signature.

FAR LEFT: Morris's "Violet and Columbine" fabric (1883).

LEFT: The "Peony" hand-painted tile, designed by Kate Faulkner for sale through Morris & Co., and registered on June 22, 1877.

RIGHT: A tile panel by Edward Burne-Jones, based on one of his favorite themes —Sleeping Beauty—for Morris & Co. in 1864.

"You might be almost as plain as Thoreau, with a rush-bottomed chair, piece of matting, and oaken trestle table; or you might have gold and lustre (the choice ware of William de Morgan) gleaming from the sideboard, and jewelled light in the windows, and walls hung with arras tapestry."

THOSE WHO ADHERED to Morris's famous maxim—"have nothing in your houses which you do not know to be useful or believe to be beautiful"—could not go wrong. When Morris delivered these words, in his 1880 lecture entitled "The Beauty of Life," he spoke directly to the new Arts & Crafts Movement. Adherents such as Ernest and Sidney Barnsley applied Morris's golden rule to the scoured and swept spaces of their whitewashed rooms, typically dominated by a sturdy oak table, around which were high ladderback chairs, and, against a far wall, an enormous dresser filled with serviceable china. Morris also lived by this rule, and his own white, paneled rooms were set off by hand-painted murals, tapestries, rich carpets, and highly patterned chintzes.

Morris both sold and owned tiles, vases, and bowls by William de Morgan, whose Iznik-inspired ceramics he valued greatly and displayed in his homes, along with a collection of blue-and-white porcelain he—like Rossetti and Whistler—had collected since the 1860s. Over fifty Chinese and Dutch pieces are displayed at

Of a certain Prince who delivered a King's daughter from a sleep of a hundred years, wherein she & all hers had been cast by enchantment

Kelmscott Manor on shelving designed by Philip Webb expressly for the purpose.

Tiles were an early staple of Morris, Marshall, Faulkner and Co., and they were sold mostly to be used as decorative panels for furniture or walls, rather than for floors. The firm brought in earthenware blanks from Holland, which were painted by, among others, Charles Faulkner's sisters Lucy and Kate, and Edward Burne-Jones's wife, Georgiana. Morris, Burne-Jones, Rossetti, Madox Brown, and Webb all contributed the designs, often based on figures or flowers. Burne-Jones made back his original £1 investment in the firm with his first four designs for tiles, and Webb was paid the decent sum of 10 shillings for his design for the "Longden" tile, which featured oak, bayleaf, and sunflower motifs, and proved to be one of the firm's most popular patterns. This tile was available in both yellow and blue and was made up into decorative inlays in cast-iron fireplace surrounds by Barnard, Bishop & Barnard. A tile panel featuring scenes from *Sleeping Beauty* was painted by Lucy Faulkner

from a design by Burne-Jones, to serve as an overmantel in the home of the Victorian watercolorist Miles Birket Foster. Morris used a Webb design of alternating swans and foliage as a tile surround for the fireplace in the Green Room at Kelmscott Manor, and William de Morgan's "Anemone" tile was used in an upstairs fireplace at Blackwell, M. H. Baillie Scott's great Arts & Crafts masterpiece in the Lake District.

A year after going into business Morris was writing to prospective clients to boast of having been "particularly successful in the revival (as we think we may call it) of the art of painting on china tiles for walls similar in manner to . . . the ancient maiolica." Morris loved the simple medieval domesticity of early Delft tiles and experimented with glazes and enamels "until the desired results were obtained."

By the 1880s and 1890s the housing boom had led to an increase in the demand for tiles—which were easily washable, hygienic, and decorative—and Morris, who had come to rely on William de Morgan

DAISY TILE (1862)

THE "DAISY" PATTERN was one of Morris's earliest and favorite motifs. He incorporated it into designs for carpets, embroideries, and wallpaper, and, in 1862, used it on what would become one of Morris, Marshall, Faulkner & Co.'s most popular tin-glazed earthenware tile. The firm sold a great many tiles, buying in handmade white Dutch blanks, which were then decorated with Morris's designs by Charles Faulkner's sisters, Kate and Lucy, or the firm's own stained-glass painters at 8 Red Lion Square before being fired again at a lower temperature in their own kilns in the basement of Red Lion Square.

The Victorian writer Aymer Vallance, writing in *The Studio*, describes how, in 1862, "Morris, Faulkner and others set about experimenting with various glazes, enamels, etc., until the desired results were obtained. An iron muffle with iron shelves carried the glass in the middle part while the tiles were so placed as to be exposed to the greatest heat, at the top and bottom. A small wind-furnace was employed for slips

and for colour-testing experiments." Sharing space in a kiln designed principally for stained glass often led to complications and failures, but did not diminish Morris's enthusiasm for producing painted tiles.

Morris took his inspiration for the humble "Daisy" and "Primrose" patterns from medieval herbals and the simple domesticity of eighteenth-century Dutch tin-glazed tiles and they proved very popular with a public increasingly aware of hygiene, who bought them in quantities to decorate their kitchens and bathrooms. Easily cleaned and durable, the firm's tiles were often incorporated into freestanding pieces of furniture, such as washstands, or made up into tile panels and used as decorative inlays in cast-iron fireplace surrounds. At the height of their popularity floral tiles, like "Daisy" or "Primrose" were used as a skirting board, to give the impression that rows of flowers were growing up out of the ground around the edges of the room.

LEFT: Four fabulous handpainted tiles by William de Morgan.

to supply the firm with tiles, found himself competing in a market dominated by the Pilkington Tile and Pottery Company, and Minton and Company. The relationship between Morris and de Morgan was a complicated one, and William de Morgan once remarked:

> "A common error is to suppose that I was a partner in Morris's firm. I was never connected with his business beyond the fact that, on his own initiative, he exhibited and sold my work, and that subsequently he employed my tiles in his schemes of decoration."

De Morgan did, however, move his ceramic works from London to Merton Abbey a year after Morris moved part of his operation up to Surrey, and the two men were not just geographically, but also artistically, close. De Morgan, like Morris, was an exceptional colorist, and he used exotic ruby reds, delicate golds, and vivid peacock blues and greens on his handmade tiles, which were inspired by the decorative patterns of early Middle Eastern wares and decorated with mythical animals, ships, birds, and plants.

Morris's strongly held belief that everyday items were worthy of an artist's or a designer's attention had the effect of elevating the status of ordinary objects and bringing beauty into the lives of ordinary people. In their own homes, he and Jane served their guests meals on Staffordshire blue and white plates —"at their table the standard of the common English Willow-pattern plate was boldly raised," wrote Georgiana Burne-Jones. This practice continued in Queen Square, where May Morris described "the look of the stately five-windowed room, with the long oak table laid for one of these dinners." "What specially attracted my attention," she recalled, "was not the old silver and blue china, but the greenish glass of delicate shapes, designed by Philip Webb . . . this gleamed like air-bubbles in the quiet candle-light and was reflected far away in the little mirrors set in the chimney-piece."

Morris & Co., who had gained such a high reputation for their stained glass, marketed a range of table glassware, based on the early drinking and wine glasses Webb had designed for Jane and William Morris to use in Red House in the early 1860s. These were Germanic in style, generously proportioned, subtle in form, and deceptively simple. They were hand-blown by skilled craftsmen at the Whitefriars Glassworks of James Powell & Sons, whose association with the firm was long and mutually beneficial. In keeping with his usual practice, Morris went to some lengths to understand the process of glassmaking, and in "The Lesser Arts of Life" (1882) he asserted:

> "In the hands of a good workman the metal is positively alive and is, you may say, coaxing him to make something pretty. Nothing but commercial enterprise capturing the unlucky man and setting him down in the glass-maker's chair with his pattern book beside him . . . could turn out ugly glasses."

The number of references to tiles and glassware being purchased or taken in payment from the firm's stock at regular intervals by Burne-Jones, Webb, and Morris himself suggests the need for regular replacements.

The enthusiasm for Arts & Crafts ceramics led to the foundation of numerous "studio" potteries and glassworks in Great Britain and the United States. The idea of an individual artist potter—as exemplified by William de Morgan, Harold Rathbone, or the eccentric American George Edgar Ohr—making individual pieces by hand from raw material to finished product, fitted in well with the philosophy of the Arts & Crafts Movement. Clay was an everyday and inexpensive material, which did not require seasoning like wood, and art potters could work quite simply, without reliance on industry or manufacturers. The closing years of the nineteenth century saw a boom in the American art pottery market, with new businesses such as the Grueby Faience Company joining the already established Fulper and Rookwood Potteries. In Great Britain, Arts & Crafts luminaries

LEFT: Philip Webb designed the firegrate, fender fire irons, and paneled surround of the fireplace in the dining room at Standen in 1894. The repoussé mild steel cheeks and smoke cowl were made by John Pearson. The grate, plate rack, and fender were created by Thomas Elsley, a London blacksmith often employed by Webb.

RIGHT: A freestanding table lamp by W. A. S. Benson in the Willow bedroom at Standen. Benson designed the table lamps to stand on bedside tables or hang from the wall. An innovator, he was the first to produce this kind of "metamorphic" fitting, which was much imitated.

such as Walter Crane and Charles Voysey leapt at the opportunity to experiment with different shapes and new luster glazes, providing designs for Pilkington's romantic "Royal Lancastrian" range.

Once again Liberty provided the retail outlet for many of the smaller art potteries, such as Moorcroft, Aller Vale, John Harrison's Linthorpe Pottery, and the Derbyshire-based Bretby Art Pottery. Liberty was where idealistic young couples who embraced Morris's ideas, but could not afford his prices, shopped. They lived in the new garden cities, where Charles Voysey's ideal of "light, bright, cheerful rooms, easily cleaned and inexpensive to keep" ornamented only by "a simple vase of flowers" was being realized. In the "Tudorbethan" store on Regent Street they could purchase the necessary ceramic pots, as well as dhurries from India, metalwork, and jewelry by some of the leading Arts & Crafts designers, and the avant-garde "Liberty Art Fabrics" popularized as the height of "Aesthetic" fashion.

The singular effect achieved by thoughtful and innovative lighting was a defining aspect of a Morris interior. Technological advances were revolutionizing the way a home was lit, and Morris often brought in his close friend W. A. S. Benson when working on large commissions. Benson, a founding member of the Art Workers' Guild, and a leading Arts & Crafts metalworker and cabinetmaker, was responsible for the slender pendant light fittings in Standen in Sussex (one of the first houses to be designed for electric lighting from the outset), and a number of other Morris & Co. commissioned interiors. His work— heavily influenced by Augustus Pugin's "Gothic" metalwork designs for simply decorated goblets, candlesticks, and lanterns—perfectly complemented the "Morrisian look" and sold so well through the firm from the mid-1880s that he was soon able to expand his Fulham workshop to include a foundry and a Kensington showroom, which he later transferred to even larger premises near Morris & Co. on New Bond Street. Benson, who also designed for the expanding furniture section of the business, patented his own reflector shades and lanterns, and took over as director of Morris & Co. on the death of Morris in 1896. His later machine-made pieces, which echoed the modernity of

Christopher Dresser and the angularity of European design, sold well in Paris through Samuel Bing's Maison de l'Art Nouveau.

The gaslit gloom of Victorian interiors was being replaced by a fresher, cleaner style, and these new forms of lighting had a profound effect on interior decoration. After years of upward-reflecting gas flames, Benson created metal shades that deflected the light downward, softening the comparatively harsh electric light, and produced a range of translucent light fittings. Early electric lamps were still relatively dim, and ceiling pendants were often suspended from pulleys so that they might be lowered when in use. Simple wood or metal frames were inset with plain etched glass or stained glass patterned with simple geometric or flowing floral motifs—seen at its most daring perhaps in the abstract patterned shades designed by Charles Rennie Mackintosh, and at its most familiar in the work of Louis Comfort Tiffany, whose leaded stained-glass light shades are an immediately recognizable icon of an authentic Arts & Crafts interior.

The fireplace was an important focal point in a Morris or an Arts & Crafts interior—"the cheerfulness we experience from the fire is akin to the delight which sunlight brings," asserted M. H. Baillie Scott—and Benson, Voysey, Ernest Gimson, and members of the Bromsgrove and Birmingham Guilds designed ironwork, and brass and copper fire accessories to sit beside the fireplace, adding to its overall decoration with gleaming fenders, firedogs, bellows, grates, and coal scuttles. Morris would have approved of the clear, clean, simple lines of contemporary fireplaces. At Red House he opted for simple red-brick chimney pieces and large freestanding grates, and in his 1880 lecture "Making the Best of It," advised his audience to do away with "wretched sham ornament" and "trumpery of cast-iron" and opt instead for "a hole in the wall of a convenient shape, faced with such bricks or tiles as will at once bear fire and clean; then some sort of iron basket in it, and out from that a real hearth of cleanable brick or tile, which will not make you blush when you look at it." In reaction to the overdecorated fireplaces of the Victorian era,

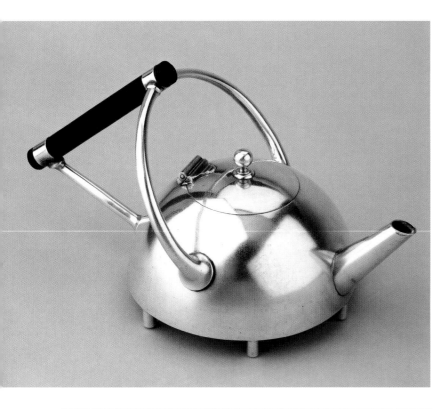

TOP LEFT: A charming electroplated hemispherical teapot on six feet, manufactured by James Dixon & Son in 1880.

BOTTOM LEFT: A lovely "Daffodil" leaded-glass and gilt bronze table lamp from the Tiffany Studios.

RIGHT: Three sturdy copper Arts & Crafts jugs.

Webb revived medieval styles and inglenook fireplaces with copper smoke hoods.

Men such as Christopher Dresser, Archibald Knox, Charles Rennie Mackintosh, and C. R. Ashbee were among the luminaries who led something of a renaissance in metalwork skills and techniques in England and Scotland at this time, while in the United States, Dirk van Erp, Gustav Stickley, and Louis Comfort Tiffany were experimenting with traditional materials such as copper, tin, and pewter, and exploring new techniques such as enameling on copper to create the distinctive rich iridescent tone that has become such a signature of the period.

The characteristic hand-hammered finish of metalwork of the period sat well in an interior where Pugin's principles of revealed construction were evident in the furniture and woodwork. Arts & Crafts metalworkers often left structural elements such as rivets or nail heads visible, in keeping with their mission to provide plain, honest decoration. The Arts & Crafts architect and designer

Ernest Gimson thought it important enough to set up the son of his local blacksmith in his own smithy so that he could oversee the metal fittings for his furniture and produce doorknobs, locks, bolts, strap hinges, candlesticks, and sconces to his own designs. Charles Voysey, too, designed his own metal fittings, from letterboxes to keyhole covers, often incorporating motifs such as birds or hearts, both of which were used in his design for the hinges on the cabinet designed to hold the Kelmscott Press edition of Chaucer's *Canterbury Tales.*

Charles Ashbee's Guild of Handicraft provided a wide variety of household items, including cutlery, tankards, bowls, salt cellars, muffin dishes, teapots, vases, candlesticks, clocks, and decorative pieces such as cigarette cases and mirror frames. These were often beautifully decorated with enamelwork, which Arthur Lazenby Liberty promptly plagiarized in his popular "Cymric" and "Tudric" lines, undercutting Ashbee's handmade items and causing Ashbee to refer to Liberty's firm thereafter as "Messrs. Nobody Novelty and Co."

In his lecture "The Beauty of Life," Morris describes his ideal room. At first this appears to be a rather spartan, scholarly space, where books take precedence, and the few chairs required must be "sturdy" and movable, but then, as he warms to his subject, he adds pictures to the room, conceding that "unless the bookcase or cupboard be very beautiful . . . you will want pictures . . . real works of art." He adds "a vase or two to put flowers in," and the entire Morris package takes shape: lusterware, lovely opalescent glass, paintings, patterns, and books. Books had always been central to Morris's idea of a civilized lifestyle. As a student he had not been able to resist "the painted books in the Bodleian," and one of his favorite pastimes had been to scour antiquarian booksellers for handsome editions to add to his growing collection or bestow as generous gifts upon friends. While still in his teens, Burne-Jones had been exceedingly grateful to find himself the recipient of a fine edition of Malory's *Morte d'Arthur*—the influence of which reverberated through his mature work.

THE KELMSCOTT CHAUCER (1896)

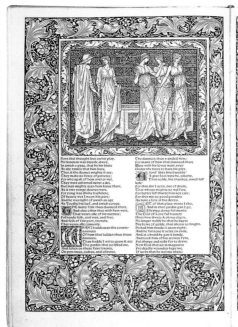

LEFT: The Kelmscott Chaucer has been described as one of the greatest English books ever produced. It is certainly one of the most beautiful.

MORRIS WAS A decorator both by profession and inclination and so, when he turned his attention to printing books, he naturally wanted to produce ones with "a definite claim to beauty." He had loved Chaucer ever since his Oxford days and, with the founding of the Kelmscott Press in a rented cottage at l6 Upper Mall, Hammersmith, in 1891, he was able to take the first steps towards realizing his cherished dream of publishing a complete edition of *The Works of Geoffrey Chaucer*. Disenchanted with the poor quality of modern printing and design, he explored ways of reviving early Renaissance methods of book production and type design. He wanted to produce a book which would "be easy to read and should not dazzle the eye, or trouble the intellect of the reader by eccentricity of form in the letters." As with all his previous enterprises, he researched his subject thoroughly and poured all his energies into producing the best possible finished books. He had ink imported from Germany, paper specially made by hand from a fifteenth-century Venetian model, and he designed three of his own typefaces—Golden, Troy, and Chaucer—based on a Roman typeface designed by Nicolaus Jenson, a fifteenth-century Venetian printer. He even designed three watermarks—flower, perch and apple—

for the handmade paper and for a while experimented with making his own ink.

The Kelmscott Chaucer—four years in the making—was a triumph. The sumptuous deluxe edition was printed on vellum with a special stamped white pigskin binding and silver clasps, and, along with the standard edition, sold out rapidly. Morris was responsible for the richly ornamented title page, the beautifully decorated initials and intricate borders which frame Edward Burne-Jones's serene illustrations. Originally, forty of these had been envisaged, though the number rose finally to eighty-seven. Morris had hoped to persuade his prim friend to tackle some of the bawdier sections in the text, but Burne-Jones chose instead to concentrate on his favorite themes of chivalry and courtly love. Nevertheless, Morris found the illustrations "magnificent and inimitable," and called them "the most harmonious decoration possible." Burne-Jones, for his part, had the highest respect for Morris's contribution, although, toward the end, he felt concerned that the "very ghostlike, feeble and old looking" Morris would not be able to finish the project and, indeed, he only just lived long enough to see the book finished in June 1896, a few months before his death in October that year.

"The mere handling of a beautiful thing seemed to give him intense physical pleasure," observed Morris's first biographer J. W. Mackail, and, at a relatively late stage in his life, Morris realized his passion for beautifully printed and bound books by setting up the Kelmscott Press and creating some of the finest examples of the period, notably the Kelmscott Chaucer, which has been described as one of the greatest English books ever produced. Printed in vellum, bound in white pigskin with silver clasps, and housed in a special cabinet designed by Charles Voysey, it took four years to produce and contained eighty-seven illustrations by Burne-Jones, as well as Morris's beautiful decorated initials and intricately patterned borders. Only 425 copies were printed, the first of which was placed in Morris's hands just three months before his death, in October 1896. The Kelmscott Press did not long outlive Morris, but its influence—as with everything else he involved himself in—was considerable.

Morris's insistence on excellence elevated standards in all areas of design, from commercial books to every aspect of the decorative arts. Above all, Morris wanted people to find pleasure in their work and take delight in their homes and their surroundings. As Nikolaus Pevsner has written, "While he followed his inborn passion for making things with his own hands, he knew also that to do this instead of painting pictures was his social duty. Before he was twenty-two, he had experimented with carving in stone and wood, moulding in clay, and illuminating. This helped him to acquire a respect for the nature of materials and working processes. Wherever he looked in contemporary industrial art, he saw manufacturers blatantly violating this. So his first furniture for his own house was nothing but a protest."

Morris urged us to take "Nature and History" as our teachers and to embrace "simplicity, everywhere, in the palace as well as in the cottage," declaring, "I do not want art for a few, any more than education for a few, or freedom for a few." His message was universal, loud, and clear, and is still relevant, accessible, and available to us today.

CASE STUDIES

RIGHT: The Great Hall, designed by Arts & Crafts architect Charles Bateman for our second case-study house—a home full of the Arts & Crafts ethos.

ALL THROUGH THE HISTORY OF interior decoration and design, fashions in color and pattern have come and gone, materials and shapes have fallen in and out of favor, but William Morris's popularity endures in a way that others before and since, however great, have not. This is in part because his patterns can be suited to modern and period houses, rural and urban settings, but the main reason is more basic than this. Although Morris called himself for preference "designer," it is his ideas, not simply his designs, that have found broad and lasting appeal. Perpetuating what he stood for is more about rejecting dross and encouraging real craftsmanship than about choosing "Willow Bough" for your bedroom curtains.

The houses featured here are scattered over a wide geographical area, from the furthest corner of Wales to central London, and from the eastern edge of Britain to the eastern edge of the United States. As you would expect, they are superficially not at all similar, but they were all built, or refashioned, by designers and architects inspired by the ideas that Morris generated. They have in common such features as unusually light, airy rooms for their time, welcoming fireplaces at the heart of the house, and a remarkable standard of craftsmanship. Even the New England houses, which can claim no direct link to Morris's influence (and one, indeed, was built before he was born), share these characteristics which have, in turn, attracted owners who value these assets and who have embraced the spirit of English Arts & Crafts.

Some of these houses have spent the intervening one hundred years or so in the hands of a series of loving owners who have recognized and treasured what they had; others have sad histories of neglect and misuse, but all are now in the care of people who truly appreciate their worth. The result is a variety of styles: some rooms overtly celebrate Morris or like-minded designers such as Charles Rennie Mackintosh, C. F. A. Voysey and Candace Wheeler; others have been painstakingly brought back to their original beauty from beneath layers of grime and paint. Some convey the feeling of a carefully preserved slice of the late nineteenth century, while others are a more modern interpretation of the Morris philosophy.

Again and again, however, they exemplify what Morris strove for: a truth to materials, and beauty and artistry in all aspects of the home. In an era of mass production, when furniture, and even whole houses, can be bought as pre-packed kits, these homeowners have sought out individual talent, commissioned work from stained-glass artists and metalsmiths, woodworkers and weavers, and even been inspired to develop their own artistic skills. Turning their back on the quick fix and shoddy workmanship, they have created homes that live up to Morris's aspiration, written two years before he died: "If I were asked to say what is at once the most important production of art and the thing most to be longed for, I should answer, 'A beautiful house.'"

AN ARTS & CRAFTS MANOR HOUSE

LEFT: Double front doors open into a spacious room that is more than just an entrance hall. This "living hall," a favorite Arts & Crafts feature, is part dining room, part casual sitting room, and is flooded with light from the upper gallery.

BELOW RIGHT: Houghton Manor seen across the back lawn.

BELOW: Sheila found this original Arts & Crafts sideboard—designed to be just the right height to carve a joint—at a local auction.

EVERY GENERATION LIKES to put its own stamp on a house, so it is very unusual to find a hundred-year-old family home with almost all its original features still intact. Not that this was immediately apparent to Sheila Scholes and her husband Gunter Schmidt when they bought Houghton Manor. The house had lain empty for two years, and for over twenty years before that had been a nursing home, subjected to intrusive safety features, easy-clean surfaces and an awful lot of black paint. But astonishingly, beneath the boarding and the gloomy paint, the floor-to-ceiling tiling and the cracked linoleum, the house's beautiful architectural details had been preserved.

Houghton Manor had been built in 1905 for a Cambridgeshire landowner, Colonel Pelley, by a local architect-turned-clergyman. The Reverend Frederick Oliphant admired the Arts & Crafts ethos, and had designed a light, airy house of fine proportions. Sheila and Gunter had contemplated decorating in a traditional style faithful to William Morris but, says Sheila, "When we saw the fine bones of the rooms emerge we decided they should be allowed to speak for themselves, rather than be swamped with colour or pattern." So they hand-stripped the floors, had the pine doors dipped, and kept furnishings as simple and natural as possible.

William Morris is closely associated with pattern, but he abhorred the "new" chemical dyes and positively rejoiced in plain surfaces. In the same spirit Sheila, who is a textile designer, has avoided dyes

ABOVE: The television room, smaller sister of the main sitting room. All of the downstairs rooms are linked with one another and similarly treated, giving the house a calm, relaxed atmosphere.

LEFT: The hammered metal fire hood in the sitting room had survived from Reverend Oliphant's day, but the fireside settles had not, so a local craftsman rebuilt them, using others in the house as a guide.

as far as possible and worked entirely with natural fabrics—unbleached cotton, raw silk, undyed linen, and wool.

Using quality materials, displaying craftsmanship rather than hiding it beneath drapes or unnecessary adornment, furnishing for comfort rather than for show, dispensing with clutter—Houghton Manor embodies all of these basic Arts & Crafts tenets, and has married the best of 1905 and 2005 in a dignified simplicity of which Morris would surely have approved.

Sheila and Gunter love the easy way in which this house works so much that they are drawing up plans to recreate it in America. What they foresee is not an exact replica, but the same layout and details to create a truly twenty-first-century Arts & Crafts house.

ABOVE: Light floods into the garden room from French windows, which lead out to the west side of the garden. Furniture here is restricted to a low wooden table and floor cushions.

RIGHT: The refectory-style table at the dining end of the hall was made by a local furniture-maker, and the chairs, while not originals, are in a suitably Arts & Crafts style.

RIGHT: All too often, bedroom fireplaces were among the earliest victims of renovation or modernization, but they survive at Houghton, and have been carefully restored. The white-painted paneling around this one is reminiscent of rooms in Morris's Red House.

FAR LEFT: As in the rest of the house, decoration in the bathroom has been kept extremely simple. The coat stand is an Arts & Crafts original, and is used for towels and bathrobes.

LEFT: Design in an Arts & Crafts house embraced everything from its basic structure to details such as door hinges and window catches. This entrancing dragon door knocker, released from layers of old paint, recalls the medieval styling favored by Morris and his colleagues.

BELOW LEFT: Soft white paintwork, stripped pine doors, and sanded and waxed floors in the bedrooms continue the theme begun in the living rooms downstairs.

A BEAUTIFULLY CRAFTED COUNTRY HOUSE

LEFT: When papering the drawing room with William Morris's "Golden Lily" (only available as a hand-blocked paper) threatened to be prohibitively expensive, the problem was ingeniously overcome by using fabric in the same design stretched taut over the walls.

RIGHT: Although a substantial farmhouse had stood here since at least the early nineteenth century, what you see today is mostly the work of Birmingham-based architect Charles Bateman.

WHEN PAUL AND CAROLYN MORGAN discovered this large house tucked away in the wilds of north-west Wales they recognized it as a home that would allow them not only to enjoy recreating Arts & Crafts interiors, but that would also happily accommodate their furniture and styles from many other eras.

The house was largely the work of Charles Bateman, commissioned in 1910 by a Mr. Gammell, who had made his wealth in South African mining. Bateman was already known as an Arts & Crafts architect, and so it is unsurprising that the plan should incorporate a Great Hall. And it is indeed great, measuring almost 50 ft (15 m) long. A number of different areas for sitting, reading, or playing create an almost intimate atmosphere, despite its size.

There was a great deal to do before the Morgans could move in in 2000—not least rebuilding eighty windows. Using local materials and skilled craftsmen rather than mass-produced goods is a principle that has guided them just as it did members of the Arts & Crafts Movement. They sought out a wealth of local talent, not only to replace the Welsh slate roof but as furniture makers, stained-glass artists, and metalworkers. Jonathan Cooke, who created the lights for the Great Hall from blackened brass and

stained glass, was a special discovery, as his father had actually lived in the house after Mr. Gammell.

The stained glass of the inner porch is a particularly fine piece of restoration work that entailed commissioning portraits from Burne-Jones originals, but also a serendipitous find. Quite by accident Paul came across the original William Morris roundels and lancet on a church floor, so sparing them from being incorporated into a modern conservatory.

Newly commissioned tables share the drawing room with traditional drop-sided Pembrokes, there are Art Deco lamps and Art Nouveau screens, the rectilinear precision of Charles Rennie Mackintosh—one bedroom is a homage to the great Scottish designer—and an occasional splash of Pugin, but in employing local craftsmanship and high-quality vernacular materials, Paul and Carolyn have achieved a sense of unity in a home full of the Arts & Crafts ethos.

ABOVE: The glowing stained glass of the inner porch incorporates salvaged William Morris designs alongside portraits after Burne-Jones: the "Prince" and the "Merchant's Daughter." The motif above the door translates as: "One step at a time."

RIGHT: On the landing several styles come together: a Victorian chaise-longue and a more modern Felix Kelly painting, a nineteenth-century copper light fitting and an ornate Pugin paper.

ABOVE: In the long Great Hall a Liberty bookcase and a high-sided Arts & Crafts armchair mix easily with locally made modern tables, traditional Turkish rugs, and distinctive Deco-style lights designed especially for the room.

LEFT: In the kitchen is another Morris pattern on the walls, this time the delicate "Sweetbriar." The Aga stove surround was carefully designed in the style of C. F. A. Voysey.

RIGHT: The unusual bookcase in the Hall is from Liberty's. The runic-looking inscription says: "Read not to believe & take for granted but to weigh & consider."

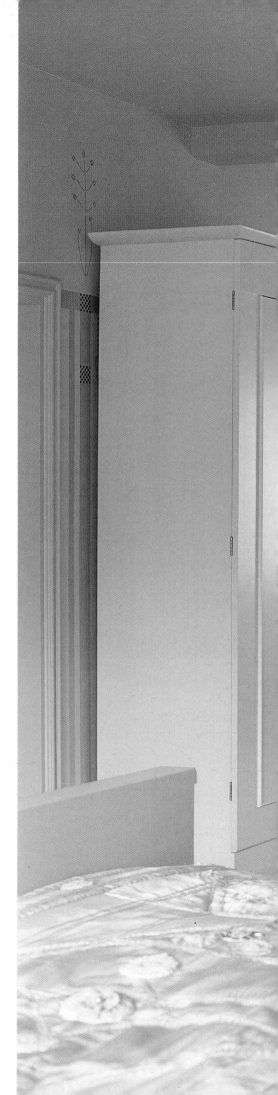

ABOVE AND LEFT: Morris's "Strawberry Thief" curtains suit this child's room, and the "thief" himself has been caught in a specially commissioned window panel.

RIGHT: The Charles Rennie Mackintosh influence is unmistakable—especially his signature rose pattern—and anyone who has visited Glasgow's Willow Tea Rooms will recognize the tall-backed chairs.

LEFT, ABOVE, AND ABOVE RIGHT:
There were plans to make this a "Voysey" bedroom in the same manner as the Mackintosh room, but chasing original Voysey furniture became an impossible dream, so pragmatism took over. Instead the Morgans worked around pieces they already owned. Both William and Jane Morris had their own four-poster beds at Kelmscott, and so it is appropriate that at least one bedroom here should have one. The fabric used for the curtains and bed hangings is a period Liberty design.

RIGHT: The Arts & Crafts influence in the drawing room is obvious, with the flat-painted plain-field paneling to dado height and William Morris wallpaper above, but the furniture ranges over several centuries, including this large Dutch display cabinet, which dates back to the late seventeenth century.

STUDY 3 A SUMPTUOUSLY DESIGNED TOWN HOUSE

POOLE'S CORNER, in Rockland, southeast of Boston, dates from the last years before machine-produced woodwork became commonplace in houses—and it is perhaps its evident individual craftsmanship that works so well with John Burrows' Arts & Crafts furnishings. John, who is only the third owner of the house since it was built for Ludo Poole in 1829, certainly feels this. "I had been looking for an old house with some character," he explains, "and was intrigued by the possibilities of a house where I could use Arts & Crafts style within earlier rooms. I was especially attracted to the hand-planed moldings of the woodwork, which are of very high quality for their time."

John's historical-design business embraces researching and reviving interior design patterns from the late nineteenth and early

OPPOSITE: The sumptuously colored dining-room carpet is Morris's "Wreath" design (c. 1876).

BELOW LEFT: Poole's Corner was built in 1829, with a sympathetic addition in 1950 by noted New England architect Charles Elliot.

BELOW: Candace Wheeler won America's first wallpaper design competition in 1881 with "Honeybee," which brings a rich yet light effect to the dining room.

twentieth centuries, and his home reflects his love of pattern and design from the period. In both the parlor and the dining room Morris-design carpets provided the starting point for the refurbishment. In the parlor he has recreated the Old Colony style of the 1880s, mixing English Arts & Crafts with American Georgian Revival. The room is filled with reminders of John's passion for the era, from the Voysey lace at the windows to a collection of late-Victorian tiles and a scene from Tennyson's "Idylls of the King"

FAR LEFT: The grandfather clock is by Keinzle of Germany, and was given to John Burrows' great-grandfather in recognition of twenty-five years of service.

ABOVE AND LEFT: But for the scenes of Cape Cod on the wall, this could be a comfortable English parlor in an "artistic home" at the turn of the last century.

by John Moyr Smith (1876) over the mantelpiece. The drape at the foot of the stairs is one of several designs in the house by Candace Wheeler, a partner of Louis Comfort Tiffany.

In the dining room (completed in 2004), John has held in check the dominance of the strikingly patterned carpet and wallpaper by having all the woodwork, including paneling and window shutters, painted a fresh white. This was a common New England treatment in the late nineteenth century, and John also discovered it recommended in Walter Crane's *Ideals in Art* (1905)—a fitting instance of good vernacular design concepts complementing each other, and a tribute to how successfully William Morris's style translates into a house built three and a half thousand miles away and seven years before Morris was born.

OPPOSITE: "Summer Street Damask," a wallpaper designed by John Dando Sedding in about 1884, acts as a soft backdrop to the eclectic mix of English, Scottish, and American furnishings and accessories.

RIGHT: Decorative tiles displayed on the mantel include examples by Morris, de Morgan, and Moyr Smith.

BELOW: Light filters into the parlor through a C. F. A. Voysey lace design called "The Stag."

STUDY 4   A SYMPATHETICALLY RESTORED MANSION

LEFT: A Morris-design carpet and wallpaper based on a Voysey pattern in the living room complement a relaxed ensemble of Arts & Crafts pieces, some original. The sharp detailing in the large fire surround was achieved using hydraulic compression bricks, which are both hard and finely textured.

"THIS HOUSE WAS TRULY A RUIN," says its owner, David Berman. "The glass was falling out of the sashes and much of the plaster had failed. I was really drawn to it." Not everyone would have been smitten by such dilapidation—"a large rotting pile," he fondly calls it—but in David it brought out excitement, not despair. He has always felt an empathy with the William Morris era, which he dates back to the schooldays in New York that he spent surrounded by Arts & Crafts architecture. Over the past decade he has sympathetically restored the many rooms, bringing back to the house the comfortable, artistic ambience it would have had when it was built, almost a century ago, for a descendant of an early settler out from England.

ABOVE: When the house was built in 1910, the shingle-hung walls and diamond windowpanes were intended to convey a colonial air.

David has strong views about working with, not against, a house's original design. Kitchens and bathrooms are often areas where period features are sacrificed to built-in convenience and twenty-first-century plumbing. Not here. The kitchen retains its original sink, a cold pantry and a butler's pantry survive, and the woodwork is southern yellow pine, favored in kitchens of the period for its high resin content and durability. David was also fortunate enough to find a 1930s stove

ABOVE, LEFT, AND RIGHT:
The stair carpet is a
William Morris pattern
known as "Lily" or "Tulip
and Lily," first produced
c. 1876. Its colors are
echoed in the Voysey
wallpaper in the hall
and stairwell, which
are lit by antique Arts &
Crafts lights.

LEFT: In the upstairs sitting room is a fine example of David's creativity: a large ceiling light in rippled and opalescent glass. He based the silhouettes, cut from patinated copper, on an Arthur Silver mermaid and a Voysey octopus.

RIGHT TOP: The little mantel clock, with its American-naïve charm and Voysey-inspired artwork, is made by David's studio.

RIGHT MIDDLE: Another of David's own lamps, drawn from a detail in a Voysey wallpaper.

RIGHT BOTTOM: Roll-top tubs survive in the bathrooms, and this one has as a backdrop an appropriately watery pattern based on a Voysey design, called "Fin and Tentacle."

just after it had been thrown out on the street; it suits his unreconstructed kitchen perfectly. The bathrooms, too, have kept their old-world charm, with roll-top tubs and exposed pipework.

Something that would have been unmistakable to any visitor to an Arts & Crafts home at the beginning of the twentieth century would have been the dedication to fine craftsmanship in every aspect of the furnishings, from the furniture and textiles to smaller details such as lampshades and picture frames. David has followed very much in this tradition. He is a talented designer, and has made many of the pieces in the house himself, from Voysey-inspired chairs to imaginative lighting. The bed pictured overleaf is his creation, as are several of the distinctive ceiling and wall lights, typically made from oak, copper, and colored glass. He also made much of the dining-room furniture—again, including the ceiling light—and framed the Chinese scroll images in the style of Leonard Wyburd, who was the in-house furniture designer at Liberty's, Regent Street. Patterns by Morris and Voysey abound, and many of the carpets were produced on the same looms used by Morris & Co. over a hundred years ago. There are indigenous echoes here, too, such as paintings by the American Arts & Crafts artist Henry Turner Bailey.

Years of benign neglect meant that modernization almost completely passed the house by. It was exactly this that attracted David to it, and has enabled him to recreate it in the Arts & Crafts spirit. As he muses, "There is very little that would not be familiar to the original owners."

ABOVE AND LEFT: On the Voysey-style bed (built by David) is a beautiful coverlet he stitched to a Voysey design. Its name, "Green Pastures," is a playful nod to "laying down in green pastures." The wallpaper is an American Arts & Crafts pattern from 1901 called "Magnolia," by Lewis Day.

RIGHT: The Voysey theme continues upstairs, both in the wallpaper on the landing walls and in the style of the ceiling light, its delicately pierced sides inspired by a Voysey music stand.

LEFT: The rescued enameled stove has a lid that closes down to give extra countertop space—an early example of providing the 1930s housewife with a sleek, modern look to her kitchen.

ABOVE: A room with many echoes of Arts & Crafts, from the Voysey wallpaper and curtains to the woven table panel and the touches of chinoiserie.

STUDY 5   A REFASHIONED FARMHOUSE

LEFT: Elements of the great entrance hall reflect the different influences in the house, from the carefully preserved linenfold panels set above the mantel, to the individual and slightly ethereal wall painting over the stairs. This twenty-first-century gift to the house was painted by an artist friend, Janet Myhill, who has included several features of the garden into the background.

RIGHT: The west wing, added by A. J. Winter Rose. In typical Arts & Crafts manner, the walls incorporate several different types of finish, including half-timbering and decorative inserts of tile and flint in the brickwork.

IN 1905 SIR HARRY COURTHOPE-MUNROE KC, Recorder of Suffolk, decided to modernize and enlarge his seventeenth-century East Anglian farmhouse. He did not have to look far for inspiration, for the village church, just next door, had been blessed with some of the best Arts & Crafts work in the region, including a Norman Shaw reredos and windows by Edward Burne-Jones, Ford Madox Brown, and William Morris himself. A. J. Winter Rose, Cambridge architect and friend of Gertrude Jekyll, undertook the sympathetic refashioning of the house, adding a whole new wing on the west side and inserting extra rooms into the original building.

Sir Harry lived here for the rest of his long life, and since then the house has had no more than two or three owners, allowing it to retain its pleasing mix of traditional Suffolk and excellent early twentieth-century craftsmanship.

This is evident as soon as you enter the huge double-height hall. It was this room, with its carved wooden staircase and large sit-in fireplace, that bowled over Robert and Kathy Janes when they first

came to the house in 2000. Robert particularly loves the magnificent ironwork on the doors and, a very Arts & Crafts touch, the precisely laid, edge-on terracotta tiles of the fireplace. He was also fascinated to discover that what he had originally scorned as that 1960s favorite, woodchip wallpaper, was in fact the effect of a local practice of mixing corn seed and husks into the plaster before applying it to the walls. He is delighted that several other rooms still show evidence of this ancient rural technique.

The large rooms have encouraged the use of bold pattern and color, such as the cobalt blue dining room and the dramatic scarlet cascade of curtains falling the entire drop of the entrance hall, but wood remains a dominant feature of the house, from the carefully waxed wood paneling and expanses of parquet flooring to furniture chosen for its quality and workmanship. Local antiques shops have yielded some good finds, but particularly striking is the specially commissioned kitchen furniture. The great table, distinctively styled chairs, and the dresser were all made for them by Scottish furniture maker Tim Stead, from elm that had fallen in the great storm which devastated homes and woodland across southern England in 1987. Many home-owners, surrounded by examples of fine craftsmanship from the past, have been inspired to seek out today's inheritors of the skills that William Morris fostered and encouraged, and the Janeses are no exception.

ABOVE: The ornate porch over the front door depicts twining grapevines, believed to be a reference to a vineyard that once grew in front of the house. The front door still carries the crest of Sir Harry Courthope-Munroe, responsible for so much of the house's layout and features.

RIGHT: The Knole sofas flanking the large inglenook fireplace were brought from a previous house, but they suit the west wing's large drawing room admirably. Designer David Porter-Hardy, with his experience of Arts & Crafts houses, provided much helpful guidance in choosing colors and creating the sort of ambience the Janeses were seeking.

LEFT: Beautifully crafted wood was a hallmark of Arts & Crafts workmanship, and the herringbone woodblock floor, paneled walls, and finely proportioned chair sum up the era. The grandfather clock commemorates the Battle of Waterloo, and was probably made in the mid nineteenth century to mark a significant anniversary of the battle.

RIGHT: In the main bedroom, simple oak furniture is complemented by the soft green of a William Morris paint ("Artichoke") and Liberty print curtains. The light two-seater with slim spindles along the back was a favorite Arts & Crafts design.

OPPOSITE AND BELOW RIGHT: This large bedroom has a wonderful view of the formal potager-style kitchen garden, laid out between miniature box hedges. Robert believes that part of the 1905 remodeling involved replacing all the windows, which have particularly fine ironwork with the sort of detailing favored by the Arts & Crafts Movement.

ABOVE: Although Aga stoves didn't appear in English kitchens until after World War I—and this one is a mere fifty years old—they have a timeless quality to them, and surely fulfill the Morris dictum: "Have nothing in your houses that you do not know to be useful or believe to be beautiful."

FAR RIGHT: The tiles here were chosen for their similarity to older existing tiles elsewhere in the house. The enormous roll-top bath, refurbished and moved from another bathroom, was probably originally installed as part of the 1905 renovation.

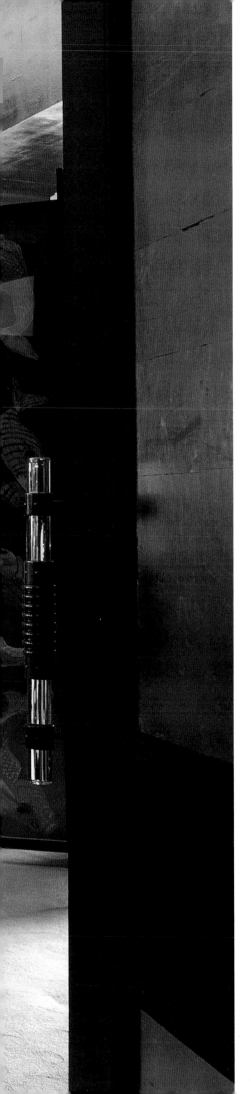

STUDY 6   A LATE-VICTORIAN TERRACED HOME

LEFT: Anthony Collett's late Victorian home is a repository for many beautifully designed pieces, although he describes himself as a hoarder rather than a "proper" collector. In the drawing room are chairs that may be attributable to E. W. Godwin and a large display of late nineteenth-century vases from the Yorkshire pottery of Burmantofts. The table, with its checkerboard *faux-marbre* top, is Anthony's own design.

RIGHT: These unusual examples from Bretby Art Pottery, which was founded in 1883, were fashioned to simulate other materials, such as wood and "gem"-studded metal.

ANTHONY COLLETT is passionate about good design. In his late nineteenth-century terraced home in west London he lives surrounded by a marvelously eclectic agglomeration of furniture, collectables, and treasures, brought together over some twenty years. However, explains Anthony, there is a common theme. "I am particularly attracted to pieces that have a strong sense of having been designed, rather than having simply evolved. Before the Arts & Crafts Movement carpenters or cabinet-makers would usually refer to pattern books or copy another piece, which meant an infinite number of variations and adaptations – often charming, but

losing distinction along the way. Morris and like-minded artists were revolutionary in instilling conscious design into everyday articles such as chairs and even detailing like door handles."

There are certainly some notably individual chairs here, from an elegant dining set that may be by the influential but often overlooked Arts & Crafts designer Edward Godwin, to a fantastical creation of bulls' horns and shaggy hide that came out of 1940s' Italy.

RIGHT: The light-filled garden studio. The simple wooden-framed furniture, typically Arts & Crafts in style, includes a double-ended chaise designed by Anthony. The selection of sinuous urns and flagons on the mantelpiece (and also the supports for the mantel shelf itself) are the work of talented metalworker Brian Fell, and the mirror behind is by another designer whose work Anthony admires—Mark Kirkley.

The wooden armchairs in the bathroom are reminiscent of Gustav Stickley's American Craftsman style in their foursquare structure and pegged joints, but they are made of an exotic hardwood that hints of origins in India or Africa.

Alongside some design highlights from a century ago—a Liberty cupboard, Burmantofts ceramics, a Fortuny lamp—are works of art that combine utility and beauty commissioned from today's talented artists: boldly shaped vases crafted in burnished mild steel by Brian Fell, a striking zinc-framed mirror and lights by Mark Kirkley, a modern version of the folding screen popular in Arts & Crafts houses. In painting the fish on the screen's glass panels the artist, Nicholaas Maritz, used a technique known as *verre églomisé*, by which the image is worked from the back and built up in reverse, with the top layer first and the background last. There are also several examples of Anthony's own work around the house, including the kitchen table and stools, bowl-like ceiling lights, and a double-ended *chaise longue*.

Perhaps the most thoroughly Arts & Crafts room, in appearance and in spirit, is, in fact, a modern addition. About ten years ago, Anthony built in his garden a square, airy studio into which natural light pours from the glazed central portion of the ceiling. The plain elm flooring, iron-banded Douglas fir columns, and the arcing roof beams, while not pretending to be other than modern, recall the medieval style favored by William Morris and his circle. Both the fine art it contains and the fabric of the room itself clearly embrace the spirit of Morris's teachings about excellence of design and truth to materials.

LEFT: The linen cupboard in the bathroom was designed for Liberty of Regent Street at the height of the Arts & Crafts period. Typically, it marries the medieval—solid oak construction, heavy iron strapwork, and basic but effective door fastenings—with the oriental, the distinctive outline subtly suggesting an old Japanese palanquin.

ABOVE: Modern art and, quixotically, a cowhide floor rug mix confidently with the Arts & Crafts ambience created by the bathroom's early twentieth-century sanitary ware and simple tongue-and-groove paneling.

ABOVE, LEFT, AND RIGHT: As well as a collection of Bretby ceramics, Anthony's drawing room is home to an extraordinary hairy chair and its zebra-striped companion table, resting next to a specially commissioned glass screen decorated by the tricky technique of "reverse painting." Beyond the screen, the bronze ceiling lamp designed by Anthony echoes a nearby umbrella lamp by Mariano Fortuny dating from c. 1910.

OPPOSITE, ABOVE, AND LEFT: The dining-room table and chairs are by Ambrose Heal, who through his family's furniture firm did so much to popularize Arts & Crafts in the early years of the twentieth century. In designing the surround for the fireplace in this room, Anthony worked with simple lines to complement the furniture, yet achieved a restrained elegance that suits a town house and the era of its contents. The mantelpiece is used to display yet more Bretby ceramics, and beside it stands a Lutyens bench.

The multi-paneled doors in the adjoining kitchen echo the patterned backs of the dining chairs and are reminiscent of Philip Webb's paneling in the drawing room and dining room at Standen, as is the high plate shelf.

WHERE TO SEE ARTS & CRAFTS

UNITED KINGDOM

CAMBRIDGESHIRE

JESUS COLLEGE
Jesus Lane, Cambridge CB5 8BL
Tel: +44 (0)1223 339339
Web: www.jesus.cam.ac.uk

The oldest college building in the city, the twelfth-century chapel at Jesus College underwent major restoration work in the nineteenth century, and in 1867 a new ceiling for the nave was designed by William Morris, and painted under his direction. In 1873–7 the windows in the nave and transepts of the chapel were glazed by William Morris, from designs by Edward Burne-Jones.

QUEENS' COLLEGE
Queen's Lane, Cambridge CB3 9ET
Tel: +44 (0)1223 335511
Web: www.quns.cam.ac.uk

The Hall features a highly decorated overmantel above the fireplace erected to the design of G. F. Bodley in 1861–2. The original tiles were designed by Morris, Burne-Jones, Rossetti, and Madox Brown, and manufactured in 1864 by Morris, Marshall, Faulkner & Co.

CUMBRIA

BLACKWELL
Bowness-on-Windermere,
Cumbria LA23 3JR
Tel: +44 (0)1539 446139
Web: www.blackwell.org.uk

M. H. Baillie Scott's masterpiece, built as a holiday home for Manchester Brewery owner Sir Edward Holt, recently restored and promoted as "the Arts & Crafts House," it includes important examples of William de Morgan tiles and furnishings from Morris & Co. Open to the public.

GLOUCESTERSHIRE

CHELTENHAM ART GALLERY AND MUSEUM
Clarence Street,
Cheltenham,
Gloucestershire GL50 3JT
Tel: +44 (0)1242 237431
Web: www.cheltenhammuseum.org.uk

Boasts a permanent exhibition of furniture by William Morris and other Arts & Crafts designers.

KELMSCOTT MANOR
Kelmscott,
Lechlade,
Gloucestershire GL7 3HG
Tel: +44 (0)1367 252486
Web: www.kelmscottmanor.co.uk

This seventeenth-century farmhouse on the banks of the Thames, near its source in Oxfordshire, became William Morris's most beloved home. Together with Dante Gabriel Rossetti he took out a joint tenancy in 1871 and spent long periods of time in the "many-gabled old house," mainly during the summers, for the house was inclined to be damp and was frequently cut off by flooded water meadows. Morris lies buried in Kelmscott churchyard beneath a gravestone designed by Philip Webb. Although not arranged exactly as Morris knew it, the house contains some notable objects associated with and related to William Morris and his family, including examples of Morris & Co. furniture, tiles, and chintzes, and is now owned by the Society of Antiquaries and, at certain times of the year, is open to the public.

RODMARTON MANOR
Cirencester, Gloucestershire GL7 6PF
Tel: +44 (0)1285 841253
Web: www.rodmarton-manor.co.uk

Ernest Barnsley designed home of Claud and Margaret Biddulph, rigorously Arts & Crafts in ethos and execution, includes many examples of notable work by Peter Waals, Alfred Powell, Sidney Barnsley, and Ernest Gimson. House and gardens open to the public.

KENT

RED HOUSE
Red House Lane,
Bexleyheath, Kent DA6 8JF
Tel: +44 (0)1494 559799
Web: www.nationaltrust.org.uk

The artistic and highly romantic home of the newly married William and Jane Morris from 1859–65. Here their two daughters, Jenny and May, were born and here they were happiest. Rossetti called it "more a poem than a house, but admirable to live in too," and contributed, as did many other friends, to the decoration of the interior. Recently restored by the National Trust.

LONDON

GEFFRYE MUSEUM
Kingsland Road, London E2 8EA
Tel: +44 (0)20 7739 9893
Web: www.geffrye-museum.org.uk

Room interiors showing English domestic styles from 1600 to the present day.

HOLY TRINITY CHURCH
Sloane Street,
Chelsea,
London SW1X 1DF
Tel: +44 (0)20 7730 7270

Richly decorated with stained glass by William Morris, Edward Burne-Jones, and Christopher Whall, and Arts & Crafts metalwork, sculpture, and other elaborate decorative details.

KELMSCOTT HOUSE

26 Upper Mall, Hammersmith,
London W6 9TA
Tel: +44 (0)20 8741 3735
www.morrissociety.org/Kelmscott_House.html

Kelmscott House, William Morris's home from 1878–96, is a private house and is not open to the public—but the basement and coach house, which are the headquarters of the William Morris Society, are open on Thursdays and Saturdays between 2pm and 5pm.

LEIGHTON HOUSE MUSEUM

12 Holland Park Road,
London W14 8LZ
Tel: +44 (0)20 7602 3316
www.rbkc.gov.uk/LeightonHouseMuseum

Former home of Frederick, Lord Leighton (1830–96), this sumptuously decorated house contains a fine collection of Victorian art, including paintings by Leighton, Burne-Jones, and Millais, along with notable tiles and ceramics by William de Morgan and a frieze by Walter Crane.

LINLEY SAMBOURNE HOUSE

18 Stafford Terrace,
Kensington,
London W8 7BH
Tel: +44(0)20 7602 3316
Web: www.rbkc.gov.uk/linleysambournehouse/

This former home of the well-known Punch cartoonist has been preserved by the Victorian Society as a glorious example of what a typical middle-class home would have looked like in the nineteenth century. The newly married Sambourne and his wife Frances were avid users of Morris wallpapers.

TATE BRITAIN

Millbank, London SW1P 4RG
Tel: +44 (0)20 7887 8000
Web: www.tate.org.uk

Contains an impressive collection of Pre-Raphaelite art, including Morris's only easel painting La Belle Iseult.

VICTORIA AND ALBERT MUSEUM

Cromwell Road, London SW7 2RL
Tel: +44 (0)20 7942 2000
Web: www.vam.ac.uk

Contains many important examples of Morris & Co. textiles, tiles, tapestries, furniture, and embroideries, as well as the Morris Room, formerly the Green Dining Room.

WILLIAM MORRIS GALLERY

Water House, Lloyd Park,
Forest Road, Walthamstow,
London E17 4PP
Tel: +44 (0)20 8527 3782
Web: www.lbwf.gov.uk/wmg

Morris's former boyhood home (1846–56) now houses the William Morris Gallery (extensive collection of works by Morris and his contemporaries) and is open to the public.

BEDFORD PARK, Chiswick, has middle-class homes designed principally by R. Norman Shaw; HAMPSTEAD GARDEN SUBURB shows how Morris's ideals were adopted by the Garden Suburb Movement.

OXFORDSHIRE

THE OXFORD UNION LIBRARY

Oxford Union,
Frewin Court, Oxford OX1 3JB
Tel: +44 (0)1865 241353

The Old Library, formerly the debating chamber, was built in 1853. It is decorated with murals by Morris, Burne-Jones, and Rossetti, and has a ceiling that was designed and decorated by Morris.

NORTHAMPTONSHIRE

78 DERNGATE

Northampton,
Northamptonshire NN1 1UH
Tel: +44 (0)1604 603407
Web: www.78derngate.org.uk

Newly restored terraced house with stunning Charles Rennie Mackintosh interior now open to the public by appointment. Formerly the home of Mr. Wenham Joseph Bassett-Lowke, a model-train manufacturer, and member of the Design and Industries Association, this proved to be the Scottish architect-designer's last commission. Open March to November.

NORTHUMBERLAND

CRAGSIDE HOUSE

Rothbury,
Morpeth,
Northumberland NE65 7PX
Tel: +44 (0)1669 620333
Web: www.nationaltrust.org.uk

The former home of Lord Armstrong, Victorian inventor and landscape architect. In the 1880s the house had hot and cold running water, central heating, fire alarms, and telephones, and was the first house in the world to be lit by electricity. Contains several bedrooms decorated with Morris wallpaper. Now a National Trust property, open to the public.

SCOTLAND

THE HILL HOUSE

Upper Colquhoun Street, Helensburgh,
Argyll and Bute G84 9AJ

Tel: +44 (0)1436 673900

Web: www.nts.org.uk

*A shining example of Charles Rennie
Mackintosh's fierce commitment to total stylistic
unity, Hill House was commissioned by the
Scottish publisher Walter Blackie in 1902.
The elongated lines and delicate geometry of
the delightful decorative schemes were a result
of a collaboration between the architect and his
wife Margaret MacDonald. Now in the care of
the National Trust for Scotland, the house and
gardens are open to the public.*

MELSETTER HOUSE

Island of Hoy,

Orkney KW16 3M2

Tel: +44 (0)1856 791352

*Designed by W. R. Lethaby in the 1890s for the
Birmingham businessman Thomas Middlemore,
and his artistically inclined wife, Theodosia, a
renowned weaver and embroiderer, who
furnished the house with Morris & Co. products.
Melsetter is now a private home, though visits
can be arranged by prior appointment.*

SUSSEX

STANDEN

West Hoathly Road,

East Grinstead, West Sussex RH19 4NE

Tel: +44 (0)1342 323029

Web: www.nationaltrust.org.uk/places/standen/

*Philip Webb designed the house for James Beale,
a successful solicitor and friend of the Ionides
family, in 1891. Beale and his wife Margaret
chose to decorate the house extensively with
Morris designs. Considered a quintessential*

*Arts & Crafts house and one of the best surviving
examples of the domestic revival, it is now owned
by the National Trust and open to the public.*

WEST MIDLANDS

BIRMINGHAM CITY MUSEUM & ART GALLERY

Chamberlain Square, Birmingham B3 3DH

Tel: +44 (0)121 303 2834

Web: www.bmag.org.uk

*Contains an important collection of Pre-
Raphaelite art and Morris & Co. works.*

WIGHTWICK MANOR

Wightwick Bank,

Wolverhampton, West Midlands WV6 8EE

Tel: +44 (0)1902 761400

Web: www.nationaltrust.org.uk

*Victorian house designed in 1887 by Edward
Ould for Theodore Mander, a wealthy paint
manufacturer, and extensively decorated with
William Morris designs—for upholstery textiles,
hangings, embroideries, and tiles—is now a
National Trust property, open to the public.*

NORTH AMERICA

CALIFORNIA

HUNTINGTON LIBRARY, ART COLLECTIONS AND BOTANICAL GARDENS

1151 Oxford Road,

San Marino, California 91108, USA

Tel: (+001) 626 405-2100

Web: www.huntington.org/ArtDiv/morris.html

*The Huntington William Morris Collection is one
of the largest research collections of full-scale
cartoons for stained glass, business documents of
the firm, designs for wallpaper, textiles, carpets,
tapestry, and embroidery, Morris drawings and
books in the world.*

CANADA

MALTWOOD ART MUSEUM & GALLERY

University of Victoria, Victoria,

British Columbia V8W 3P2 Canada

Tel: (+001) 250 721-6562

Web: www.maltwood.uvic.ca

*The Maltwood Bequest of fine, decorative and
applied arts includes works of William Morris
and the English Arts & Crafts Movement, housed
primarily at the Maltwood Collection Study Gallery.*

DELAWARE

THE DELAWARE ART MUSEUM

2310 Kentmere Parkway,

Wilmington, Delaware 19806, USA

Tel: (+001) 302 571-9590

Web: www.delart.org

*The Samuel and Mary R. Bancroft Pre-Raphaelite
Collection includes important early furniture by
William Morris and Dante Gabriel Rossetti, and
a Viking Ship stained-glass panel by Morris & Co.*

ILLINOIS

GLESSNER HOUSE MUSEUM

1800 South Prairie Avenue,

Chicago, Illinois 60616, USA

Tel: (+001) 312 326-1480

Web: www.glessnerhouse.org

*A masterpiece by architect H. H. Richardson, this
Romanesque Revival townhouse from 1887 has
restored interiors decorated extensively with
products from Morris & Co.*

MAINE

SARAH ORNE JEWETT HOUSE

5 Portland Street,

South Berwick, Maine 03908, USA

Historic New England (SPNEA)

Tel: (+001) 207 384-2454

Web: www.historicnewengland.org

Several rooms of Georgian home of author Sarah Orne Jewett were decorated using Morris & Co. carpet and Arts & Crafts wallpapers in the late nineteenth century. These interiors are a superb example of Morris style in an eighteenth-century American house.

MASSACHUSETTS

TRINITY CHURCH

Copley Square,

Boston,

Massachusetts 02116, USA

Tel: (+001) 617 536-0944

Web: www.trinityboston.org

A Romanesque church completed in 1876, and designed by H. H. Richardson, contains the greatest collection of stained glass by Morris & Co. and Edward Burne-Jones in America.

RHODE ISLAND

CHATEAU-SUR-MER

474 Bellevue Avenue,

Newport, Rhode Island 02840, USA

The Preservation Society of Newport County

Tel: (+001) 401 847-1000

Web: www.newportmansions.org

Chateau-sur-Mer was built in 1852 and 1872 (Richard Morris Hunt, architect). Mr. George Peabody Wetmore's bedroom survives intact from the 1870s with wallpaper by William Morris and Jeffrey & Co.

WISCONSIN

VILLA LOUIS

St. Feriole Island,

521 North Villa Louis Road,

Prairie du Chien,

Wisconsin 53821, USA

Wisconsin Historical Society

Tel: (+001) 608 326-2721

Web: www.wisconsinhistory.org/villalouis

An Italaniate mansion built on the Mississippi River in 1870. In 1885 Hercules Louis Dousman redecorated the house with the aid of J. J. McGrath, an agent for William Morris in Chicago. The Morris and Wardle wallpapers and textiles in Pre-Raphaelite colorings have all been carefully reproduced during a recent restoration.

HELP & ADVICE

UNITED KINGDOM

THE VICTORIAN SOCIETY

1 Priory Gardens,

London W4 1TT

Tel: +44 (0)20 8994 1019

Web: www.victoriansociety.org.uk

Arts and Crafts-related events and lectures; also visits to private houses not normally open to the public.

THE WILLIAM MORRIS SOCIETY

Kelmscott House, 26 Upper Mall,

Hammersmith, London W6 9TA

Tel: +44 (0)20 8741 3735

Web: www.morrissociety.org

Visits, lectures, and social events. Their website has details of events in the USA as well as the United Kingdom.

NORTH AMERICA

THE ARTS & CRAFTS SOCIETY

1194 Bandera Drive,

Ann Arbor, MI 48103, USA

Tel: (+001) 734 358 6882

Web: www.arts-crafts.com

Events calendar and online marketplace.

WILLIAM MORRIS SOCIETY OF CANADA

87 Government Road,

Toronto,

Ontario, M8X 1W4, Canada

Tel: (+001) 416 233 7686

Web: www.wmsc.ca

Visits, lectures, and social events.

SPECIALIST SUPPLIERS

UNITED KINGDOM

ABBOT JONES DESIGN PARTNERSHIP
The Outbuildings,
Fron Dirion,
Mynydd Mechel, Amlwch,
Anglesey LL68 0TE
Tel: +44 (0)1407 710 928

Stained glass (as featured in Case Study 2).

THE ANTIQUE TRADER/ THE MILLINERY WORKS
87 Southgate Road,
Islington, London N1 3JS
Tel: +44 (0)20 7359 2019
Web: www.millineryworks.co.uk

Specializing in furniture and effects of the Arts & Crafts Movement.

ART FURNITURE
158 Camden Street,
London NW1 9PA
Tel: +44 (0)20 7267 4324
Web: www.artfurniture.co.uk

Original furniture, metalwork, lighting, and some textiles.

THE ARTS AND CRAFTS FURNITURE COMPANY
49 Sheen Lane,
London SW14 8AB
Tel: +44 (0)20 8876 6544

Original furniture, lighting, ceramics, fabrics, carpets, and pictures.

THE ARTS AND CRAFTS HOME
25A Clifton Terrace,
Brighton, Sussex BN1 3HA
Tel: +44 (0)1273 327 774 for mail order
Web: www.achome.co.uk

Fine replicas of furniture, lighting, carpets, and accessories, as well as a range of wallpaper fabrics and original pieces.

CHRISTIE'S SOUTH KENSINGTON
85 Old Brompton Road, London SW7 3LD
Tel: +44 (0)20 7581 7611
Web: www.christies.com

Twentieth-century decorative art and design sales.

CLASSICAL GLASS
Woodstock, Llanrwst Road, Glan Conwy,
Gwynedd LL28 5SR
Tel: +44 (0)i492 580 454

(As featured in case Study 2).

COLE & SON
Chelsea Harbour Design Centre,
Lots Road, London SW10 0XE
Tel: +44 (0)20 7376 4628

Hand-blocked wallpapers to order, including some by Owen Jones who influenced Morris. Also many other beautiful Arts & Crafts designs.

JONATHAN COOKE
Nantcol Works, Llanbedr,
Gwynedd LL45 2NP
Tel: +44 (0)1341 241 587

Lamps and metalwork (as featured in Case Study 2).

THE COUNTRY SEAT
Huntercombe Manor Barn,
Nr Henley on Thames, Oxfordshire RG9 5RY
Tel: +44 (0)1491 641349
Web: www.the countryseat.com

Architect-designed furniture from the nineteenth and twentieth centuries, related art pottery, metalwork, and glass.

THE FINE ART SOCIETY
148 New Bond Street, London W1Y OJT
Tel: +44 (0)20 7629 5116

A gallery selling nineteenth- and twentieth-century fine and decorative arts, including Arts & Crafts furniture, fabrics and accessories.

BERNARD HARMAN
Also at Nantcol Works (see Jonathan Cooke)
Tel: +44 (0)1341 241 587

Welsh oak furniture (as featured in Case Study 2).

HASLAM AND WHITEWAY
105 Kensington Church Street,
London W8 7LM
Tel: +44 (0)20 7229 1145

Nineteenth-century British design, including Arts & Crafts. Stock can include tiles, stained-glass windows, furniture, and even fireplaces.

THE HOUSE 1860–1925
6-10 St James Street,
Monmouth, Monmouthshire NP25 3DL
Tel: +44 (0)1600 712 721
Web: www.thehouse1860-1925.com

Large collection of Arts & Crafts and period countryhouse furniture; website offers an online ordering facility.

MARK KIRKLEY
Tel/ Fax: +44 (0)1424 812 613

Designer and manufacturer of interior metalwork (as featured in Case Study 2).

LIBERTY & CO.
210/220 Regents Street, London W1R 6AH
Tel: +44 (0)20 7734 1234

Original Arts & Crafts furniture, as well as reproduction pieces. Don't miss its annual Arts & Crafts selling exhibition.

PAUL REEVES

32b Kensington Church Street,
London W8 4HA
Tel: +44 (0)20 7937 1594

Top-quality Arts & Crafts furniture and accessories.

PHILLIPS

101 New Bond Street, London W1Y 0AS
Tel: +44 (0)20 7629 6602

Twentieth-century decorative art and design sales.

JEAN SALT

Tel: +44 (0)1766 770 801

Embroidery and hangings (as featured in Case Study 2).

SANDERSON

Tel: +44 (0)1895) 251288 for stockists
Web: www.sanderson-uk.com

Bought Morris & Co.'s wallpaper printing blocks when it closed. Morris's designs still feature in its range; some are hand-printed in original colors from original blocks. Also Morris designed printed fabrics.

SOTHEBY'S

34/35 New Bond Street, London W1A 2AA
Tel: +44 (020) 7293 5000
Web: www.sothebys.co.uk

Twentieth-century decorative art and design sales.

WOODWARD GROSVENOR & CO. LTD.

Sourvale Mills, Green Street,
Kidderminster, Worcestershire DY10 1AT
Retail sales enquiries: 01562 513500
(USA contact: J. R. Burrows & Company)

The weavers of authentic Morris Wilton carpets and stair runners—they have continued this line since around 1900, when they were the carpet weavers for Morris & Co.

NORTH AMERICA

CHARLES RUPERT

2005 Oak Bay Avenue, Victoria,
British Columbia V8R 1E5 Canada
Tel: (+001) 250 592-4916
Web: www.charlesrupert.com

William Morris wallpaper and fabric, along with other English Arts & Crafts designs.

DESIGNS IN TILE

Box 358,
Mount Shasta, California 96067, USA
Tel: (+001) 530 926 2629
Web: www.designsintile.com

William Morris tiles.

FAMILY HEIRLOOM WEAVERS

Show House, June Pond Farm,
775 Meadowview Drive,
Red Lion, Pennsylvania 17356, USA
Tel: (+001) 717 246-2431
Web: www.familyheirloomweavers.com

William Morris ingrain carpet (mail order, retail).

J. R. BURROWS & COMPANY

393 Union Street, P.O. Box 522,
Rockland, Massachusetts 02370, USA
Tel: (+001) 800 347-1795; (+001) 781 982-1812
Web: www.burrows.com

William Morris Wilton and Brussels carpet and the Burrows Studio line of English Arts & Crafts wallpaper (mail order, retail, trade, appointment only). (As featured in Case Study 3).

BURROWS STUDIO SHOWROOM

12 Masonic Place,
Provincetown, Massachusetts 02657, USA
Tel: (+001) 508 487-3848
Web: www.burrows.com

English Arts & Crafts wallpaper, including designs of John Dando Sedding, Aldam Heaton and C. F. A. Voysey Art At Home Gallery (open spring, summer, fall).

OSBORNE & LITTLE INC.

Tel: (+001) 212 751-3333
www.osborneandlittle.com
(for a complete list of showrooms in North America)

Libertys Furnishing Fabrics, including English Arts & Crafts fabric.

SANDERSON (as above)

New York Showroom (trade only)
979 Third Avenue, Suite 409,
New York, New York 10022, USA
Tel: (+001) 212 319-7220
Web: www.sanderson-uk.com
(for a complete list of showrooms in North America)

SCALAMANDRE

Tel: (+001) 212 980-3888
Web: www.scalamandre.com
(for a complete list of showrooms in North America)

William Morris woven and printed fabric and wallpaper, along with designs by Thomas Wardle.

TRUSTWORTH STUDIOS

Trustworth Studios, Box 1109,
Plymouth, Massachusetts 02362, USA
Tel: (+001) 508 746-1847
Web: www.trustworth.com

English Arts & Crafts wallpaper and Wellspring textiles, including designs of C. F. A. Voysey (mail order, retail, trade). (As featured in Case Study 4).

BIBLIOGRAPHY

Angeli, Helen, *Rossetti, Dante Gabriel Rossetti, His Friends and Enemies*, Hamish Hamilton, 1949

Arts and Crafts Essays by members of the Arts and Crafts Exhibition Society, with a Preface by William Morris, Longmans, Green & Co., 1899

Ashbee, C. R., *The Guild of Handicraft*, Essex House Press, 1909

Bradley, Ian, *William Morris and His World*, Thames and Hudson, 1978

Brandon Jones, John, *William Morris and Kelmscott*, London Design Council, 1981

Bryson, John (with Janet Camp Troxell), *Dante Gabriel Rossetti and Jane Morris, Their Correspondence*, Clarendon Press, 1976

Burne-Jones, Georgiana, *Memorials of Edward Burne Jones* (2 volumes), Macmillan, 1904

Carruthers, Annette and Mary Greensted, *Good Citizen's Furniture, The Arts & Crafts Collections at Cheltenham*, Cheltenham Art Gallery and Museums in associations with Lund Humphries, 1994

Cobden-Sanderson, T. J., *The Arts and Crafts Movement*, Hammersmith Publishing Society, 1905

Crane, Walter, *The Bases of Design*, G. Bell & Sons, 1898

Crane, Walter, and F. Day Lewis, *Moot Points, Friendly Disputes on Art and Industry*, London, 1903

Day, Lewis F. *Nature and Ornament*, Batsford, 1909

Eastlake, Sir Charles, *Hints on Household Taste*, London, 1865

Faulkner, Peter, *Against the Age: An Introduction to William Morris*, Allen and Unwin, 1980

Faulkner, Peter and Peter Preston (eds), *William Morris Centenary Essays*, University of Exeter Press, 1999

Fitzgerald, Penelope, *Edward Burne Jones: A Biography*, Michael Joseph, 1975

Harris, Jennifer, *William Morris and the Middle Ages*, Manchester University Press, 1984

Harvey, Charles and Jon Press, *William Morris Design and Enterprise in Victorian Britain*, Manchester University Press, 1991

Heal's Catalogue 1853–1934, Middle Class Furnishings, David and Charles, 1973

Henderson, Philip, *The Letters of William Morris to his Family and Friends*, Longmans, Green & Co., 1950

Hollamby, Edward, *Red House*, Architecture, Design and Technology Press, 1991

Jekyll, Gertrude with Lawrence Weaver, *Gardens for Small Country Houses*, Country Life Limited, 1912

Jones, Owen, *The Grammar of Ornament*, Day & Son, 1856

Kelmscott Manor: An Illustrated Guide, The Society of Antiquaries, 1996

Kelvin, Norman, *The Collected Letters of William Morris* (4 volumes), Princeton University Press, 1984-1996

Lago, Mary, *Burne-Jones Talking*, John Murray, 1982

Lethaby, W. R., *Philip Webb and his Work*, Oxford University Press, 1935

Lubbock, P (ed.), *Letters of Henry James*, London, 1920

MacCarthy, Fiona, *William Morris, A Life for Our Time*, Faber and Faber, 1994

Mackail, J. W., *The Life of William Morris* (2 volumes), Longmans, Green & Co., 1899

Marsh, Jan, *Jane and May Morris, A Biographical Story 1839–1938*, Pandora, 1986

Morris & Co. Decorators 1861–1940 A Commemorative Centenary Exhibition Catalogue, The Arts Council, 1961

Morris, May, *Introduction to the Collected Works of William Morris*, reprinted in 2 vols, Oriole Editions, 1973

Morris, William, *Collected Works of William Morris* (24 volumes, edited by May Morris), Longmans, Green & Co., 1910–15

Morris, William, *News from Nowhere*, originally published in *The Commonweal, January-October 1890*, first English edition Reeves and Turner, 1891

Morris, William, *Hopes and Fears for Art, Five Lectures Delivered in Birmingham, London, and Nottingham, 1878-1881*, Ellis & White, 1882

Naylor, Gillian, *William Morris by Himself, Designs and Writings* Macdonald, 1988

Parry, Linda, *William Morris*, Philip Wilson Publishers, in association with The Victoria and Albert Museum, 1996

Parry, Linda, *William Morris Textiles*, Weidenfeld and Nicolson, 1983

Pevsner, Nikolaus *Pioneers of the Modern Movement from William Morris to Walter Gropius*, Faber & Faber, 1936

Poulson, Christine (ed), *William Morris on Art & Design*, Sheffield Academic Press, 1996

Pugin, A. W. N., *The True Principles of Pointed or Christian Architecture*,

London 1843, reprinted by Academy Editions, 1973

Robertson, W. Graham, *Time Was*, Hamish Hamilton, 1931

Robinson, William, *The English Flower Garden*, John Murray 1883

Rose, Phyllis, *Parallel Lives, Five Victorian Marriages*, Chatto and
Windus, 1984

Rossetti, William Michael, *Pre-Raphaelite Diaries and Letters*,
Hurst and Blackett Limited, 1900

Rossetti, William Michael, *Some Reminiscences*, Brown Langham &
Co Ltd. 1906

Ruskin, John, *The Seven Lamps of Architecture*, George Allen, 1894

Ruskin, John, *The Stones of Venice*, 2 volumes, Allen & Unwin, 1904

Smith, Grey and Sarah Hyde, eds., *Walter Crane 1845-1915,
Artist, Designer and Socialist*, Lund Humphries, 1989

Stansky, Peter, *William Morris*, Oxford University Press, 1983

Stanksy, Peter, *Redesigning the World: William Morris, the 1880s and
the Arts and Crafts*, Princeton University Press, Princeton,
New Jersey, 1985

Stickley, Gustav, *Craftsman Homes: Architecture and Furnishings
of the American Arts and Crafts Movement, 1909*, reprinted
Dover Publications, 1979

Surtees, Virginia (ed.), *The Diary of Ford Madox Brown*,
Yale University Press, 1981

Thirkell, Angela, *Three Houses*, Oxford University Press, 1932

Todd, Pamela, *The Sweet Days Die, Poems by William Morris*,
Pavilion Books, 1996

Todd, Pamela, *The Pre-Raphaelites at Home*, Pavilion Books, 2001

Todd, Pamela, *The Arts & Crafts Companion*, Thames & Hudson, 2004

Walkley, Giles *Artists' Houses in London 1764–1914*, Scolar Press, 1994

Watkinson, Raymond, *William Morris as Designer*, Studio Vista, 1967

Wilhide, Elizabeth, *William Morris: Decor & Design*, Pavilion, 1991

ACKNOWLEDGMENTS

Many people have helped me in the preparation and writing of this book. I acknowledge with thanks the facilities afforded me by the British Library, the University of London libraries, the Victoria and Albert Museum, the Tate Gallery and the Courtauld Institute. I would like to take this opportunity to specially thank the Trustees of the London Library for their grant and acknowledge the unfailingly courteous help and assistance of the many librarians in reference sections of London borough libraries who have rallied to my aid, as have the guides and custodians of Red House, Kelmscott Manor, Standen, Wightwick and the William Morris Gallery at Walthamstow. I am grateful to them all. I should also like to thank David Fordham for designing the book so beautifully; Kate Brunt for finding the modern locations on this side of the Atlantic and John Burrows for finding them in America, Chris Tubbs for photographing them all, and Caroline Ball for writing the text to accompany them. I am deeply grateful to Emily Hedges for researching the pictures so calmly at such an exciting period of her life; to Hilary Hanslip for showing interest in the project at every stage; to Mark Golding; Mikyla Bruder and Lisa Campbell at Chronicle for their involvement; to Sonya Newland, Beverley Jollands and Victoria Webb at Palazzo for safely and expertly guiding the book through the editorial process and to Colin Webb—William Morris's greatest fan—for commissioning me to write it in the first place.

PAMELA TODD

With special thanks to John Burrows for his assistance as US consultant.

The publishers would like to thank all the owners and designers who generously allowed us to photograph their homes and work for this book.

J.R. Burrows & Company (*see Specialist Suppliers*); David E. Berman, Trustworth Studios (*see Specialist Suppliers*); Collett-Zarzycki Ltd., 2B Fernhead Road, London W9 3ET, Tel: +44 (0020 8969 6967; David Porter Hardy Interiors Ltd., Tel: +44 (0)1728 627 953; Sheila Scholes, www.sheilascholes.co.uk, Tel: +44 (0)1480 498 241

PICTURE ACKNOWLEDGMENTS

The publishers would like to thank the following sources for their kind permission to reproduce the photographs and illustrations in this book.

Key
BAL = The Bridgeman Art Library
NTPL = The National Trust Photographic Library
V&A = The V&A Picture Library
WMGL = The William Morris Gallery, London

Pages 5, 19, 30–31, 41–43, 46, 93, 109, 127–179, 192 Chris Tubbs

Page 1 V&A, 2 Jeremy Cockayne/arcaid.co.uk, 3 V&A, 6 NTPL/Nadia Mackenzie, 7 National Portrait Gallery, 8 and 9 V&A, 10 WMGL, 11–13 V&A, 14 Jonathan Buckley, 15 l V&A, 15 r WMGL, 16 and 17 V&A, 18 WMGL, 20 NTPL/Andrew Butler, 21 and 22 V&A, 23 NTPL/Andrew Butler, 24 Jonathan Buckley, 25 NTPL/Andrew Butler, 26 V&A, 27 NTPL/Nadia Mackenzie, 28 V&A, 29 Society of Antiquaries of London, 32–33 James Mortimer/Interior Archive, 34 BAL/Mallett Gallery, London, UK, 35 Jerry Harpur/Gravetye Manor. Designer William Robinson, 36 NTPL/Michael Caldwell, 37 and 38 V&A, 39l NTPL/Nadia Mackenzie, 39r National Monuments Record, 40 V&A, 44 V&A, 45 WMGL, 47 Jeremy Cockayne/ arcaid.co.uk, 48–49 Jeremy Cockayne/arcaid.co.uk, 50 V&A, 51 NTPL/Andreas von Einsiedel, 52 James Mortimer/Interior Archive, 53 The Oxford Union Society, 54 Christie's Images Ltd, 55 Blackwell The Arts and Crafts House, 56 NTPL/Andreas von Einsiedel, 57–60 V&A, 61 NTPL/Andreas von Einsiedel, 62 V&A, 63 The Society of Antiquaries of London, 64 NTPL/Michael Caldwell, 66 WMGL, 67 Richard Bryant/arcaid.co.uk, 68–71, V&A, 72 James Mortimer/ Interior Archive, 73 NTPL/Derrick E Witty, 74–77 V&A, 78 and 79 Jeremy Cockayne/arcaid.co.uk, 80–81 NTPL/Andreas von Einsiedel, 82 V&A, 83 NTPL/Nadia Mackenzie, 84 Christie's Images Ltd, 85 Alan Weintraub/arcaid.co.uk, 86 Christie's Images Ltd, 87 Fritz von der Schulenburg/Interior Archive, 88 V&A, 89 Christie's Images Ltd, 90 NTPL/Andreas von Einsiedel, 91 National Portrait Gallery, 92 V&A, 94 Castle Howard Estate Ltd, 95–98 V&A, 99 NTPL/Nadia Mackenzie, 100 and 101 V&A, 102l Kevin A. Lataday, 102–104 V&A, 105 WMGL, 106–108 V&A, 110 Richard Bryant/ arcaid.co.uk, 111–114 V&A, 115 Angelo Hornak Library, 116l V&A, 116r BAL/Private Collection, 117 NTPL/Roy Fox, 118 NTPL/Michael Caldwell, 119 NTPL, 120 and 121 NTPL/Andreas von Einsiedel, 122t BAL/Private Collection, 122b Corbis/Christie's Images Ltd, 123 Fritz von der Schulenburg/Interior Archive, 124 V&A, 125 Delaware Art Museum, F. V. du Pont Acquisition Fund, 126 NTPL/Derrick E. Witty

INDEX